EASY LOW-FAT 60
BAKING
RECIPES

EASY LOW-FAT
BAKING 60 RECIPES

Healthy and delicious low-fat, low-cholesterol cookies, scones, cakes and breads, shown step by step in more than 300 beautiful photographs

Consultant Editor **Linda Fraser**

southwater

This edition is published by Southwater,
an imprint of Anness Publishing Ltd, Blaby Road,
Wigston, Leicestershire LE18 4SE

Email: info@anness.com

Web: www.southwaterbooks.com; www.annesspublishing.com

© Anness Publishing Ltd 2011

If you like the images in this book and would like to investigate
using them for publishing, promotions or advertising, please visit
our website www.practicalpictures.com for more information.

Publisher: Joanna Lorenz
Editor: Linda Fraser
Production Controller: Christine Ni

PUBLISHER'S NOTE

Front cover shows Strawberry Roulade – for recipe, see page 23

ETHICAL TRADING POLICY

Because of our ongoing ecological investment programme, you, as our
customer, can have the pleasure and reassurance of knowing that a tree
is being cultivated on your behalf to naturally replace the materials
used to make the book you are holding. For further information about
this scheme, go to www.annesspublishing.com/trees

Previously published as part of a larger volume,
Low-Fat Baking

NOTES

Bracketed terms are intended for American readers.
For all recipes, quantities are given in both metric and imperial
measures and, where appropriate, in standard cups and spoons.
Follow one set of measures, but not a mixture, because they are
not interchangeable.
Standard spoon and cup measures are level. 1 tsp = 5ml,
1 tbsp = 15ml, 1 cup = 250ml/8fl oz.
Australian standard tablespoons are 20ml. Australian readers should
use 3 tsp in place of 1 tbsp for measuring small quantities.
American pints are 16fl oz/2 cups. American readers should use
20fl oz/2.5 cups in place of 1 pint when measuring liquids.
Electric oven temperatures in this book are for conventional ovens.
When using a fan oven, the temperature will probably need to be
reduced by about 10–20°C/20–40°F. Since ovens vary, you should
check with your manufacturer's instruction book for guidance.
The nutritional analysis given for each recipe is calculated per portion
(i.e. serving or item), unless otherwise stated. If the recipe gives a range,
such as Serves 4–6, then the nutritional analysis will be for the smaller
portion size, i.e. 6 servings. The analysis does not include optional
ingredients, such as salt added to taste.
Measured quantities of fat or oil in lists of ingredients do not include
fat or oil used to grease baking trays or pans.
Medium (US large) eggs are used unless otherwise stated.

CONTENTS

Introduction

When we talk of cakes and baking we tend to imagine rich, calorie-laden treats that are well out of reach if you are following a low-fat diet. With reduced-fat cooking methods, however, it is very easy to create delicious, low-fat cakes, cookies and breads that are full of flavour and appeal. It is generally agreed that a high-fat diet is bad for us – especially if the fats are of the saturated variety – but unless you are making meringues or angel cakes, it is rarely possible to do without any fat whatsoever in baking.

The good news is that it is possible to cut down considerably on the amount of fat used, and equally good results can be achieved using healthier unsaturated oils instead of saturated fats. Polyunsaturated oils such as sunflower oil, corn oil and safflower oil are excellent for most baking purposes, as is olive oil, which is an example of an oil that is monounsaturated. Olive oil is good for recipes that require a good, strong flavour. When oil is not suitable, for example when you need a light airy result, choose a soft margarine that is high in polyunsaturates. Low-fat spreads are ideal for spreading but not good for baking, because they contain a high proportion of water.

Although cheese is high in saturated fat, its flavour makes it invaluable in many recipes. Choose either reduced-fat or half-fat varieties with a mature flavour, or a lesser amount of a highly flavoured cheese such as Parmesan. There is no need to use full cream (whole) milk – try skimmed milk or fruit juice instead. Buttermilk (the liquid left over from churning butter) is, surprisingly, virtually fat-free and is perfect for soda bread and scones. Cream undoubtedly adds a touch of luxury to special occasion cakes, and it is high in fat, but fromage frais, thick yogurt or curd cheese sweetened with honey make delicious low-fat fillings and toppings for even the most elaborate cakes.

Using healthier fats in baking enables you to make scrumptious cakes and other treats that look and taste every bit as good as those made traditionally with butter and cream. The recipes in this book are sure to inspire, impress and amaze all those who thought that the concept of low-fat baking was too good to be true.

Left: Everyone loves fresh breads, scones and biscuits hot from the oven, and you don't have to sacrifice flavour when you use reduced-fat cooking techniques.

Store Cupboard

Cutting down on fat doesn't mean sacrificing taste. Instead, choose basic ingredients that are naturally lower in fat. This is not so limiting as it sounds, as the following suggestions show.

FLOURS

Mass-produced, highly refined flours are fine for most baking purposes, but for the best results choose organic stone-ground flours because they will add flavour as well as texture.

Rye flour

This dark-coloured flour has a low gluten content and gives a dense, flavoursome loaf. It is best mixed with wheat flour to give a lighter loaf.

Soft flour

Sometimes called sponge flour, it has less gluten than plain (all-purpose) flour and is ideal for light cakes and biscuits.

Strong bread flour

Made from hard wheat which contains a high proportion of gluten, this flour is used for bread-making.

Wholemeal (whole-wheat) flour

Because this flour contains the complete wheat kernel, it gives a coarser texture and a good, wholesome flavour to bread.

NUTS AND SEEDS

Most nuts are low in saturated fats and high in polyunsaturated fats. Use them sparingly as their total fat content is high. Sunflower seeds, linseeds and poppy seeds add texture.

YEAST

Yeast helps bread to rise, whether fresh or dried, regular or easy-blend (rapid rise).

HERBS AND SPICES

Chopped fresh herbs can enhance the taste of breads, scones and soda breads. In the absence of fresh herbs, dried herbs can be used: less is needed but the flavour is generally not as good.

Spices can add strong or subtle flavours depending on the amount used. Ground cinnamon, freshly grated nutmeg and mixed spice are widely used in baking but more exotic spices, such as saffron or cardamom, can add distinctive flavour. To ensure they are fresh, buy herbs and spices in stores where you know there is a high turnover. Because they lose flavour over time, it is always better to buy small amounts of herbs and spices.

SWEETENERS

Dried fruits

A wide range of fruit is available, including varieties such as peach, pineapple, banana and mango, as well as the more familiar currants and glacé (candied) cherries. Natural sugars in dried fruits add sweetness to bakes and keep them moist, so you can use less fat.

Fruit juice

Concentrated fruit juices are very useful for baking. They have no added sweeteners or preservatives and can be diluted as required. Use them in their concentrated form for baking or for sweetening fillings.

Honey

Good honey has a strong flavour so you can use rather less of it than the equivalent amount of sugar. It also contains traces of minerals and vitamins.

Malt extract

A sugary by-product of barley, malt extract has a strong flavour and adds moisture to bread, cakes and teabreads.

Molasses

The residue left after the first stage of refining sugar cane, molasses has a strong, smoky and slightly bitter taste and adds a moist texture to bakes and cakes. Black treacle, a blend of refinery syrup and molasses, can be used as a substitute.

Pear and apple or other fruit spreads

This is a concentrated fruit juice with no added sugar. It can be used as a spread or blended with fruit juice and added to recipes as a sweetener.

Unrefined sugars

Choose unrefined sugars rather than refined sugars for baking, as they have more flavour and contain some minerals.

Right: It's easier to reduce fat when you are cooking if you have a store cupboard full of tempting ingredients, such as fresh fruits, dried fruits, eggs, sugar, grains, spices and herbs. All of these can be used for baking and are naturally low in fat.

Fat and health

A small amount of fat is essential for health and well-being; fat is a valuable source of energy and also makes food more palatable. However, lowering your intake of fats, especially saturated fats, will reduce the risk of developing certain diseases, and help you to lose weight and increase energy levels.

All fats in foods are made from the building blocks of fatty acids and glycerol, and their properties vary according to each combination.

Two types of fat are found in food – saturated and unsaturated. The unsaturated group is further divided into two types – polyunsaturated and monounsaturated fats.

A combination of the three types of fat (saturated, polyunsaturated and monounsaturated fats) are found naturally in most foods, but the amount of each type varies greatly from one food to another.

SATURATED FATS

Fatty acids are made from chains of carbon atoms. Each atom has one or more so-called free 'bonds' that link with other atoms; in this way the fatty acids transport nutrients to cells in the body. Without these free 'bonds' the carbon atom cannot form any links; it is completely 'saturated'. As a result, the body finds it difficult to process the fatty acid into energy, consequently it is stored by the body as fat.

Saturated fats should be eaten sparingly, because they can increase the level of cholesterol in the blood, which in turn can increase the risk of developing heart disease.

The main sources of saturated fats are animal products, such as meat, and butter and lard, which are solid at room temperature. However, there are also saturated fats of vegetable origin – such as coconut and palm oils, and some hard margarines and oils, which are processed by changing some of the unsaturated fatty acids to saturated ones – these are labelled 'hydrogenated vegetable oil' and should be avoided. These fats are present in many ready-made foods.

POLYUNSATURATED FATS

There are two types of polyunsaturated fats: those of vegetable or plant origin (omega 6), such as sunflower oil, soft margarine and seeds; and those from oily fish (omega 3), such as herring, mackerel and sardines. Both fats are usually liquid at room temperature. Small quantities of polyunsaturated fats are essential for good health and may help reduce cholesterol levels.

MONOUNSATURATED FATS

Found in foods such as olive oil, rapeseed oil, some nuts such as almonds and hazelnuts, oily fish and avocados, monounsaturated fats are known as good fats. This is because when eaten in moderation, they are believed to lower the blood cholesterol level. This quality may be the explanation of the low incidence of heart disease in some Mediterranean countries.

CUTTING DOWN FATS

When making your own cakes, scones, breads, cookies and muffins, it is fairly easy to cut down on obvious sources of fat in the diet, such as butter, oils, margarine, cream, whole milk and full-fat cheese, by substituting healthier ingredients, and switching to low-fat alternatives.

By being aware of foods that are high in fats and particularly in saturated fats, and by making simple changes when you are cooking, you can still supply your body with all the nutrients it needs for optimum health, while reducing the total fat content of your diet quite considerably.

Above: *Hazelnut oil is perfect for baking as it adds a nutty flavour to sweet dishes.*

Above: *Corn oil is ideal for recipes when a strong taste is not needed.*

Above: *Macadamia oil is light but its flavour is good with chocolate and sweet dishes.*

Reducing fat in baking

There are many simple ways of cutting down the amount of fat you use in baking. Saturated fats such as butter or lard can be replaced by unsaturated alternatives, such as vegetable oils, and nonstick cookware and baking parchment also help keep fat levels to a minimum.

Some low-fat or reduced-fat ingredients and products work better than others in cooking, but often a simple substitution of one for another works perfectly.

Instead of butter, margarine and hard fats, use low-fat spread or polyunsaturated margarine. However, very low-fat spreads with a fat content of 20% or less have a high water content and so are unsuitable for baking because, unlike butter, they will not make a cake with a light and airy texture.

If a recipe calls for full-fat products such as whole milk, cream, butter, hard margarine, crème fraîche, whole milk yogurts and hard cheese, substitute semi-skimmed or skimmed milk and milk products, low-fat yogurts, low-fat fromage frais and low-fat soft cheeses, reduced-fat hard cheeses such as Cheddar, and reduced-fat creams and crème fraîche.

For scones or pastries, avoid hard cooking fats, such as lard or hard (hydrogenated) margarine, and choose the healthier option of polyunsaturated or monounsaturated oils, such as olive, sunflower or corn oil, instead. Rather than use full-fat milk, cream or yogurt, try alternative fat-free or low-fat ingredients for all your baking and cooking. Choose fruit juice, low-fat or fat-free stock, wine or even beer to add flavour without the fat.

Above: *Foods that contain the three main types of fats: Oily fish (polyunsaturated fats); butter (saturated fat); nuts, almond oil, olive oil, rapeseed (canola) oil, sunflower oil and avocado oil (monounsaturated fats).*

Above: *Wine can be used instead of full-fat milk. The alcohol evaporates during cooking.*

Above: *Fruit juice is fat-free and can be used instead of fattier liquids such as milk or cream.*

Above: *Beer, as well as adding flavour, acts as a raising agent in batters, and it is fat-free.*

Oils, Fats and Dairy Produce

Although some fats are unsuitable for baking, there are many alternatives suggested here. While eggs have cholesterol and saturated fat in the yolks, current thinking is that healthy adults can enjoy eggs in baked foods without an increased risk of heart disease.

LOW-FAT OILS AND FATS

Low-fat spreads are ideal for spreading on breads and teabreads, but are not suitable for baking because of a high water content. When you are baking, try to avoid saturated fats such as butter and hard margarine. Use oils high in polyunsaturates such as corn, sunflower or safflower oil. Choose margarine that is high in polyunsaturates.

Low-fat spread, rich buttermilk blend
This is made with a high proportion of buttermilk, which is naturally low in fat. It is unsuitable for baking.

Olive oil
Use monounsaturated extra virgin olive oil when a strong flavour is required.

Olive oil reduced-fat spread
Based on olive oil with a good flavour, it is not suitable for baking.

Reduced-fat butter
This contains about 40% fat; the rest is water and milk solids emulsified together. It is not suitable for baking.

Very low-fat spread
Contains only 20–30% fat and so is not suitable for baking.

Sunflower light
Not suitable for baking, it is only 40% fat, plus emulsified water and milk solids.

Sunflower oil
High in polyunsaturates, this is an oil that can be used for many baked recipes because it has a pleasant, but not too dominant flavour.

LOW-FAT CHEESES

There are many low-fat cheeses that can be used in baking. Generally, harder cheeses have a higher fat content than soft cheeses. Choose mature (sharp) cheese as you will need less of it to give a good flavour.

Cottage cheese
A low-fat soft cheese that is also available in a half-fat form.

Curd (farmers') cheese
A fresh low-fat soft cheese that is a form of cottage cheese, from which the liquid has been removed, it is made with either skimmed or semi-skimmed milk. It can be used instead of cream cheese.

Edam and Maasdam
Two medium-fat hard cheeses well suited to baking.

Feta cheese
This is a medium-fat cheese with a firm, crumbly texture. It has a slightly sour, salty flavour.

Half-fat Cheddar and Red Leicester
These contain about 14% fat.

Mozzarella light
This is a medium-fat version of an Italian soft cheese.

Quark
Made from fermented skimmed milk, this soft, white unriped cheese is virtually fat-free. it can be used as a substitute for sour cream.

CREAM ALTERNATIVES

Yogurt and fromage frais make excellent alternatives to cream, and combined with honey, liqueurs or other flavourings make delicious fillings or toppings for bakes.

Bio yogurt
This contains bacterial cultures that can aid digestion. Bio yogurt has a mild, sweet taste.

Crème fraîche
This thick soured cream has a mild, lemony taste. Half-fat crème fraîche has a fat content of 15%.

Fromage frais
This soft cheese is available as virtually fat free (0.4% fat), and a more cream variety (7.9% fat).

Greek (US strained plain) yogurt
This thick, creamy yogurt is made from whole milk with a fat content of 10%. A low-fat version is also available.

Above: Sunflower oil is high in polyunsaturates and is reported to help lower cholesterol.

Above: Pistachio oil is a monounsaturated oil, rich in vitamin E. It adds good flavour to cakes.

Above: Extra virgin olive oil is full of flavour, and it is a healthy monounsaturated fat.

Above: There is a whole range of lower-fat cheeses that can be used in baking.

Right: Use low-fat milks for baking, and yogurt or fromage frais as an alternative to cream.

LOW-FAT MILK

Buttermilk
Made from skimmed milk with a bacterial culture, it is very low in fat.

Powdered skimmed milk
A useful, low-fat store cupboard standby.

Semi-skimmed milk
With a fat content of only 1.5–1.8%, this milk tastes less rich than full-cream milk. It is favoured by many people for everyday use for precisely this reason.

Skimmed milk
This milk has had virtually all the fat removed, leaving only 0.1–0.3%.

EGGS
These are essential for baking. Egg yolks are an emulsifier and help to create a fine texture, while the whites add structure.

Baking tools and equipment

Although it is possible to make do with a few multi-purpose kitchen utensils, it is better to invest in quality equipment if you intend to bake on a regular basis. A good selection of moulds, cutters, tins (pans) and interesting paper liners will add an extra dimension to your baking.

Baking parchment
This can be used for lining cake or muffin tins (pans).

Baking sheet
Choose a large, heavy baking sheet that will not warp at high temperatures.

Balloon whisk
Used for whisking egg whites and incorporating air into other mixtures.

Box grater
This multi-purpose grater can be used for citrus rind, fruit, vegetables and cheese.

Brown paper
This may be used for wrapping around the outside of cake tins (pans) in order to protect the cake mixture from the full heat of the oven and to stop the sides of the cake from burning.

Cake tester
A simple implement, rather like a very fine skewer that, when inserted into a cooked cake, will come out clean if the cake is ready.

Cook's knife
This has a heavy, wide blade and is ideal for chopping.

Deep round cake tin (pan)
Ideal for baking both rich and light fruit cakes or when a large sandwich cake is required.

Electric whisk
Ideal for creaming cake mixtures, whipping cream or whisking egg whites.

Grater
A box cheese grater is perfect for grating hard cheese as well as a variety of vegetables. This type of grater can also be used if grated chocolate is required in a recipe. For best results, chill the chocolate overnight in the refrigerator before you begin to grate it.

Honey twirl
This is specially designed to spoon honey without dripping.

Juicer
Made from porcelain, glass or plastic – used for squeezing the juice from citrus fruits.

Kitchen scissors
Keep scissors in your working area and use them specifically for culinary purposes, such as snipping bacon and fresh herbs into muffin batters and, of course, cutting paper liners and snipping pastry.

Knives
A palette knife (metal spatula) is useful for smoothing buttercream and frostings over the tops of cakes and muffins and for loosening pies, tarts and breads from baking sheets. A sharp-pointed knife can be used to cut shapes around paper templates placed on rolled-out cookie dough.

Loaf tin (pan)
Available in various sizes and used for making loaf-shaped breads, teabreads and cakes.

Measuring jug (cup)
Absolutely essential for measuring any kind of liquid accurately.

Measuring spoons
Standard measuring spoons are essential for measuring small amounts of liquid or solid ingredients. Use either UK or US measures, but not both.

Left: Basic baking equipment: weighing scales, measuring jug (cup), balloon whisk, wire rack, measuring spoons, whisk, wooden spoon, small sieve (strainer), mixing bowls and box grater.

Mixing bowls
A set of different-sized bowls is essential for whisking and mixing ingredients.

Muffin tin (pan)
These are available in aluminium or silicone materials. The muffin cups are wider at the top than at the bottom, or they may be taller with straight sides. Muffins baked in either shape of tin use the same paper cases and take the same amount of time to bake. Individual dariole moulds are used to make tall, slim muffins.

Nutmeg grater
This miniature grater is used for grating whole nutmegs.

Paper cases
The finely folded muffin cases are convenient for easy release, help to keep muffins fresher for longer, and mean less washing up of sticky tins for the cook. In the absence of a muffin tin, treble the paper cases (one inserted inside the other) and bake the muffins free-standing on a baking sheet in the oven. Dariole moulds or tall, slim muffin tins should be lined with pleated cake cases cut to size from paper liners used for loaf tins.

Pastry brush
Useful for brushing excess flour from pastry and for brushing glazes over pastries, breads and tarts.

Pastry (cookie) cutters
These are available in all shapes and sizes to make decorations for cakes, cookies and muffins, or for cutting out rounds.

Right: *For easy, low-fat cooking, non-stick bakeware is ideal because it is unlikely to need greasing before use, or only a small amount of fat will be needed to prevent sticking.*

Choose metal rather than plastic cutters so you achieve well-defined shapes. Decorative cutters can be purchased from specialist cookware shops, or you may find a larger selection if you search the internet.

Piping (pastry) bags
These are used for piping buttercreams and other creamy frostings. Large piping bags are usually made from fabric and fitted with large plastic nozzles that can easily be washed, dried and reused. Ready-made, disposable piping bags made of baking parchment are used to pipe thin lines for small decorations. Snip off the tip of the bag for an instant nozzle.

Rectangular cake tin (pan)
For making tray cakes and bakes, served cut into slices.

Ring mould
Perfect for making angel cakes and other ring-shaped cakes.

Sandwich cake tin (pan)
Ideal for sponge cakes; make sure you have two the same size.

Sieves (strainers)
Use a sieve for sifting flours with raising agents, or for sifting out any lumps from icing (confectioners') sugar. Use a smaller tea strainer when straining brewed coffee. A large wire sieve (strainer) is ideal for most normal baking purposes, while a nylon sieve is suitable for most baking purposes, but particularly for sieving acidic ingredients that may cause off-flavours in the food when they react with the metal.

Square cake tin (pan)
Used for making square cakes or cakes to be served cut into smaller squares.

Swiss roll tin (jelly roll pan)
This shallow tin is designed specifically for Swiss rolls.

Vegetable knife
A useful knife for preparing any fruit and vegetables that you may add to your recipes.

Wire rack
Place baked items on the rack for cooking, to allow circulation of air, and prevent them becoming too moist.

Wooden spoon
Essential for mixing ingredients and creaming mixtures.

Weighing scales
Invest in a set of scales to weigh precise quantities. Use either imperial or metric measurements, but never a combination of the two.

CAKES

Low in fat doesn't have to mean low in enjoyment.
These deliciously light cakes are full of fruits, nuts and spices.
You'll discover flavours suited to all seasons and occasions.
Family and friends will never believe that healthy low-fat
food could taste this good.

Spiced Date and Walnut Cake

Nuts and dates are a classic flavour combination in this easy low-fat, high-fibre cake.

SERVES 10

300g/11oz/2²⁄₃ cups wholemeal
    (whole-wheat) self-raising
    (self-rising) flour
a pinch of salt
10ml/2 tsp mixed (apple pie) spice
150g/5oz/¾ cup chopped dates
50g/2oz/½ cup chopped walnuts
60ml/4 tbsp sunflower oil
115g/4oz/½ cup muscovado
    (molasses) sugar
300ml/½ pint/1¼ cups skimmed milk
walnut halves, to decorate

Nutritional information	
Calories	265kcals/1114kJ
Fat	9.27g
Saturated fat	1.14g
Cholesterol	0.6mg
Fibre	3.51g

1 Preheat the oven to 180°C/350°F/ Gas 4. Grease and line a 900g/2lb loaf tin (pan) with baking parchment, then lightly grease the paper.

2 Sift together the flour, salt and spice, returning any bran from the sieve (strainer). Stir in the chopped dates and walnuts.

3 Mix the oil, sugar and milk together in a separate bowl. Add the oil mixture to the dry ingredients, then stir to combine thoroughly.

4 Spoon into the prepared tin and arrange the walnut halves on top. Bake the cake for about 45–50 minutes, or until golden and firm. Turn out the cake, remove the lining paper and leave to cool on a wire rack.

Variation

Pecan nuts can be used in place of the walnuts in this cake.

Greek Honey and Lemon Cake

This cake is wonderfully moist and tangy, and makes a delicious tea-time treat.

MAKES 16 SLICES

40g/1½oz/3 tbsp sunflower margarine
60ml/4 tbsp clear honey
finely grated rind and juice of 1 lemon
150ml/¼ pint/⅔ cup skimmed milk
150g/5oz/1¼ cups plain (all-purpose) flour
7.5ml/1½ tsp baking powder
2.5ml/½ tsp freshly grated nutmeg
50g/2oz/⅓ cup semolina
2 egg whites
10ml/2 tsp sesame seeds

Nutritional information

Calories	82kcals/342kJ
Fat	2.62g
Saturated fat	0.46g
Cholesterol	0.36mg
Fibre	0.41g

3 Sift the flour, baking powder and nutmeg into the bowl with the melted mixture and stir to combine thoroughly. Gradually beat in the semolina. Whisk the egg whites in a separate clean bowl until they form soft peaks, then, using a large metal spoon, fold them evenly into the mixture.

4 Spoon the mixture into the tin and sprinkle the top with the sesame seeds. Bake the cake for 25–30 minutes, until golden brown. Mix together the reserved honey and lemon juice and drizzle over the cake while warm. Cool in the tin, then cut the cake into 16 fingers to serve.

1 Preheat the oven to 200°C/400°F/ Gas 6. Lightly grease a 19cm/7½in square deep cake tin (pan) and line the base with baking parchment.

2 Place the margarine and 45ml/3 tbsp of the honey in a pan, and heat gently until melted. Reserve 15ml/1 tbsp lemon juice, then stir in the rest with the rind and milk. Transfer to a large mixing bowl.

Cook's Tip

A Lenten version of this cake uses oil as a substitute for the margarine.

Irish Whiskey Cake

This moist, rich fruit cake is drizzled with whiskey as soon as it comes out of the oven.

SERVES 12

115g/4oz/½ cup glacé (candied) cherries

175g/6oz/¾ cup muscovado
   (molasses) sugar

115g/4oz/⅔ cup sultanas (golden raisins)

115g/4oz/⅔ cup raisins

115g/4oz/⅔ cup currants

300ml/½ pint/1¼ cups cold tea

300g/11oz/2⅔ cups self-raising
   (self-rising) flour, sifted

1 egg

45ml/3 tbsp Irish whiskey

Nutritional information

Calories	265kcals/1115kJ
Fat	0.88g
Saturated fat	0.25g
Cholesterol	16mg
Fibre	1.48g

1 Mix the cherries, sugar, dried fruit and tea in a large bowl. Leave to soak overnight until all the tea has been absorbed into the fruit. Preheat the oven to 180°C/350°F/ Gas 4.

2 Grease and line a 1kg/2¼lb loaf tin (pan). Add the flour, then the egg to the fruit mixture and beat thoroughly until well mixed.

3 Pour the mixture into the prepared tin and bake for 1½ hours or until a skewer inserted into the centre of the cake comes out clean.

4 Prick the top of the cake with a skewer and drizzle over the whiskey. Stand for 5 minutes, then remove from the tin and cool on a wire rack.

Cook's Tip

If time is short, use hot tea and soak the fruit for just 2 hours.

Fruit and Nut Cake

This rich fruit cake is best left to mature for at least two to three weeks before cutting.

SERVES 12–14

175g/6oz/1½ cups self-raising (self-rising)
  wholemeal (whole-wheat) flour
175g/6oz/1½ cups self-raising
  (self-rising) flour
10ml/2 tsp mixed (apple pie) spice
a pinch of salt
15ml/1 tbsp apple and apricot or
  other fruit spread
45ml/3 tbsp clear honey
15ml/1 tbsp black treacle (molasses)
90ml/6 tbsp sunflower oil
175ml/6fl oz/¾ cup orange juice
2 eggs, beaten
675g/1½lb/4 cups mixed dried fruit
45ml/3 tbsp split almonds
50g/2oz/¼ cup glacé (candied)
  cherries, halved

1 Preheat the oven to 160°C/325°F/ Gas 3. Grease and line a deep round 20cm/8in cake tin (pan). Using string or tape, secure a band of brown paper around the outside.

2 Sift the flours into a large mixing bowl with the mixed spice, and salt and make a well in the centre.

3 Put the apple and apricot spread in a small bowl. Gradually stir in the honey and black treacle. Add to the dry ingredients with the oil, orange juice, eggs and mixed fruit. Stir together well.

4 Turn the mixture into the prepared tin and smooth the surface. Arrange the almonds and cherries in a pattern over the top. Bake for 2 hours or until a skewer inserted into the centre comes out clean.

5 Stand the tin on a wire rack until cold, then lift the cake out of the tin and remove the paper. Store for up to 3 months wrapped in baking parchment, then in foil, in a cool, dry place.

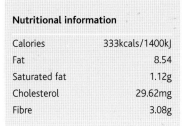

Nutritional information	
Calories	333kcals/1400kJ
Fat	8.54
Saturated fat	1.12g
Cholesterol	29.62mg
Fibre	3.08g

Apricot and Orange Roulade

This elegant dessert is good served with a spoonful of yogurt or crème fraîche.

SERVES 6

4 egg whites

115g/4oz/generous ½ cup golden caster (superfine) sugar

50g/2oz/½ cup plain (all-purpose) flour

finely grated rind of 1 small orange

45ml/3 tbsp orange juice

10ml/2 tsp icing (confectioners') sugar and shredded orange rind, to decorate

For the filling

115g/4oz/½ cup dried apricots

150ml/¼ pint/⅔ cup orange juice

Nutritional information

Calories	203kcals/853kJ
Fat	10.52g
Saturated fat	2.05g
Cholesterol	0mg

1 Preheat the oven to 200°C/400°F/ Gas 6. Grease and line a 23 x 33cm/ 9 x 13in Swiss roll tin (jelly roll pan). Grease the baking parchment.

2 For the roulade, place the egg whites in a large bowl and whisk them until they hold peaks. Gradually add the sugar, whisking hard between each addition.

3 Fold in the flour, orange rind and juice. Spoon the mixture into the prepared tin and spread it evenly.

4 Bake for about 15–18 minutes, or until the sponge is firm and light golden in colour. Turn out on to a sheet of baking parchment and roll it up Swiss (jelly) roll-style loosely from one short side. Leave to cool.

5 For the filling, roughly chop the apricots, and place them in a pan with the orange juice. Cover and leave to simmer until most of the liquid has been absorbed. Purée the apricots in a food processor or blender.

6 Unroll the roulade and spread with the apricot mixture. Roll up, arrange strips of paper diagonally across the roll, sprinkle lightly with lines of icing sugar, remove the paper and sprinkle with shredded orange rind to serve.

Strawberry Roulade

This light roulade is made with a soufflé-type mixture rolled around a low-fat creamy fruit filling.

SERVES 6

4 egg whites

115g/4oz/generous ½ cup golden caster (superfine) sugar, plus extra for sprinkling

75g/3oz/⅔ cup plain (all-purpose) flour, sifted

30ml/2 tbsp orange juice

115g/4oz/1 cup strawberries, chopped

150g/5oz/⅔ cup low-fat fromage frais or low-fat cream cheese

strawberries, to decorate

Nutritional information	
Calories	154kcals/646kJ
Fat	0.24g
Saturated fat	0.01g
Cholesterol	0.25mg
Fibre	0.61g

2 Place the egg whites in a large bowl and whisk until they form soft peaks. Gradually whisk in the sugar. Fold in half of the sifted flour, then fold in the rest with the orange juice.

4 Sprinkle a sheet of baking parchment with the sugar. Turn out the cake on to the parchment. Peel off the paper. Roll up the sponge from one short side, with the paper inside. Cool.

1 Preheat the oven to 200°C/400°F/ Gas 6. Grease a 23 x 33cm/9 x 13in Swiss roll tin (jelly roll pan) and line with baking parchment.

3 Spoon the mixture into the prepared tin, spreading evenly. Bake for 15–18 minutes, or until golden brown and firm to the touch.

5 Unroll and remove the paper. Stir the strawberries into the fromage frais and spread over the sponge. Re-roll and decorate with strawberries.

Banana and Ginger Parkin

The combination of banana and ginger gives a new slant to this traditional recipe.

3 Spoon into the tin and bake for about 1 hour, or until firm to the touch. Allow to cool in the tin, then turn out and cut into squares.

4 Sift the icing sugar into a bowl and stir in just enough water to make a smooth, runny icing. Using a piping (pastry) bag, drizzle the icing over each square and top with a piece of stem ginger, to decorate.

SERVES 12

200g/7oz/1¾ cups plain (all-purpose) flour
10ml/2 tsp bicarbonate of soda (baking soda)
10ml/2 tsp ground ginger
150g/5oz/1¼ cups medium oatmeal
60ml/4 tbsp muscovado (molasses) sugar
75g/3oz/6 tbsp sunflower margarine
150g/5oz/⅓ cup golden (light corn) syrup
1 egg, beaten
3 ripe bananas, mashed
75g/3oz/¾ cup icing (confectioners') sugar
preserved stem ginger, to decorate

1 Preheat the oven to 160°C/325°F/ Gas 3. Grease and line an 18 x 28cm/ 7 x 11in cake tin (pan).

2 Sift together the flour, bicarbonate of soda and ginger, then stir in the oatmeal. Melt the sugar, margarine and syrup in a pan, then stir into the flour mixture. Beat in the egg and mashed bananas.

Nutritional information

Calories	277kcals/1163kJ
Fat	6.9g
Saturated fat	1.4g
Cholesterol	16.4mg

Cook's Tips

This is a nutritious, energy-giving cake that is a really good choice for packed lunches as it doesn't crumble easily. The parkin keeps very well and improves with time. It can be stored in a tightly sealed container for up to two months.

Cranberry and Apple Ring

Tangy cranberries add an unusual flavour to this low-fat cake. It is best eaten very fresh.

SERVES 8

225g/8oz/2 cups self-raising
   (self-rising) flour
5ml/1 tsp ground cinnamon
75g/3oz/scant ½ cup light muscovado
   (brown) sugar
1 crisp eating apple, cored and diced
75g/3oz/½ cup fresh or frozen cranberries
60ml/4 tbsp sunflower oil
150ml/¼ pint/⅔ cup apple juice
apple slices dipped in lemon juice, and
   cranberry jelly, to decorate

1 Preheat the oven to 180°C/350°F/
   Gas 4. Lightly grease a 1 litre/
1¾ pint/4 cup ring mould with oil.

2 Sift together the flour and ground
   cinnamon, then stir in the sugar.

3 Toss together the diced apple
   and cranberries. Stir into the
dry ingredients, then add the oil
and apple juice and beat well.

4 Spoon the mixture into the prepared
   ring mould and bake for about
35–40 minutes, or until the cake is firm
to the touch. Turn out and leave to
cool completely on a wire rack.

5 Just before serving, decorate the cake
   with apple slices, then drizzle with
warmed cranberry jelly.

Nutritional information

Calories	202kcals/848kJ
Fat	5.91g
Saturated fat	0.76g
Cholesterol	0mg
Fibre	1.55g

Cook's Tips

Fresh cranberries are available throughout
the winter months and if you don't use
them all at once, they can be frozen for
up to a year. This ring would be an ideal
alternative to Christmas cake for those
who prefer something lighter. It would
be a good way of using up any leftover
cranberries or cranberry jelly.

Cinnamon Apple Gateau

This lovely moist gateau, topped with honey-sweetened apples, makes a perfect sweet treat.

SERVES 6

3 eggs
115g/4oz/generous ½ cup caster
    (superfine) sugar
75g/3oz/⅔ cup plain (all-purpose) flour
5ml/1 tsp ground cinnamon

For the filling and topping

4 large eating apples
60ml/4 tbsp clear honey
15ml/1 tbsp water
75g/3oz/½ cup sultanas (golden raisins)
2.5ml/½ tsp ground cinnamon
350g/12oz/1½ cups low-fat soft
    (farmer's) cheese
45ml/3 tbsp reduced-fat fromage frais or
    natural (plain) yogurt
10ml/2 tsp lemon juice
45ml/3 tbsp apricot glaze (see Cook's Tip)
mint sprigs, to decorate

Nutritional information

Calories	203kcals/853kJ
Fat	10.52g
Saturated fat	2.05g
Cholesterol	0mg
Fibre	2.53g

Cook's Tip

Apricot glaze is useful for brushing over a fresh fruit topping or filling. Place a few spoonfuls of apricot jam in a small pan along with a squeeze of lemon juice. Heat the jam, stirring until it is melted and runny. Pour the melted jam into a wire sieve (strainer) set over a bowl. Stir the jam with a wooden spoon to help it go through the sieve. Return the strained jam to the pan. Keep the glaze warm until needed, then brush it over the cake.

1 Preheat the oven to 190°C/375°F/ Gas 5. Grease and line a 23cm/9in sandwich tin (layer cake pan). Place the eggs and caster sugar in a bowl and whisk until thick and mousse-like.

2 Sift the flour and cinnamon over the egg mixture and fold in with a metal spoon. Pour into the tin and bake for 25–30 minutes or until the cake springs back when pressed. Turn out to cool on a wire rack.

3 To make the filling, peel, core and slice three of the apples and put them in a pan. Add 30ml/2 tbsp of the honey and the water. Cover and cook over a gentle heat for about 10 minutes. Add the sultanas and cinnamon, stir well, replace the lid and leave to cool.

4 Put the soft cheese in a bowl with the remaining honey, the fromage frais or yogurt and half the lemon juice. Beat until the mixture is smooth.

5 Halve the cake horizontally, place the bottom half on a board and drizzle over any liquid from the apples. Spread with two-thirds of the cheese mixture, then top with the apple filling. Fit the top of the cake in place.

6 Using a palette knife, swirl the remaining cheese mixture over the top of the sponge. Core and slice the remaining apple, sprinkle with lemon juice and use to decorate the edge of the cake. Brush the apple with the apricot glaze and place mint sprigs on top, to decorate.

Carrot Cake with Lemon Frosting

Lemon frosting makes a tangy topping for this delicious all-time favourite.

4 Mix the liquids, then stir into the dry ingredients. Whisk the egg whites until stiff, then fold in evenly. Spoon into the tin and bake for 45–50 minutes.

5 Insert a cocktail stick (toothpick) or a fine skewer in the centre of the cake. If it is cooked, the cocktail stick will come out clean.

6 Turn out and cool on a rack. For the frosting, beat the cheese, lemon rind and honey until smooth. Spread over the cake. Decorate with lemon rind.

SERVES 8

2 medium carrots
225g/8oz/2 cups self-raising (self-rising) wholemeal (whole-wheat) flour
10ml/2 tsp ground allspice
115g/4oz/½ cup light muscovado (brown) sugar
50g/2oz/⅓ cup sultanas (golden raisins)
75ml/5 tbsp sunflower oil
75ml/5 tbsp orange juice
75ml/5 tbsp skimmed milk
2 egg whites

For the frosting

175g/6oz/¾ cup skimmed milk soft (farmer's) cheese
finely grated rind of ½ lemon
30ml/2 tbsp clear honey
shredded lemon rind, to decorate

2 Peel and trim the carrots, then grate them using the fine side of the grater. Set aside.

1 Preheat the oven to 180°C/350°F/ Gas 4. Grease a deep 18cm/7in round cake tin (pan) with a little of the oil, and line the base with a circle of baking parchment.

3 Sift the flour and spice together, then stir in the sugar, grated carrots and sultanas.

Nutritional information	
Calories	272kcals/1146kJ
Fat	7.72g
Saturated fat	1.04g
Cholesterol	0.4mg
Fibre	3.33g

Angel Cake

A delicious light cake that can be served with tea or coffee or as a dessert for any special occasion.

SERVES 10

40g/1½oz/⅓ cup cornflour (cornstarch)
40g/1½oz/⅓ cup plain (all-purpose) flour
8 egg whites
225g/8oz/generous 1 cup caster (superfine) sugar,
    plus extra for sprinkling
5ml/1 tsp vanilla extract
90ml/6 tbsp glacé icing, made with 115g/4oz icing
(confectioner's) sugar and 15ml/1 tbsp orange juice
5 physalis and icing (confectioners') sugar, to decorate

1 Preheat the oven to 180°C/350°F/ Gas 4. Sift both flours on to a sheet of baking parchment.

4 Sprinkle baking parchment with caster sugar and set an egg cup in the centre. Invert the cake tin over the paper, balancing it on the egg cup. When cold, the cake will drop out of the tin. Transfer it to a plate, spoon over the glacé icing, arrange the physalis on top, dust with icing sugar and serve.

Nutritional information	
Calories	139kcals/582kJ
Fat	0.08g
Saturated fat	0.1g
Cholesterol	0mg
Fibre	0.13g

2 Whisk the egg whites in a large, grease-free bowl until very stiff, then gradually add the sugar and vanilla extract, whisking until the mixture is thick and glossy.

3 Gently fold in the flour mixture with a large metal spoon. Spoon into an ungreased 25cm/10in angel cake tin (pan), smooth the surface and bake for about 45–50 minutes, until the cake springs back when lightly pressed.

Lemon Chiffon Cake

There is a tangy lemon mousse filling in this light cake, which is surprisingly low in fat.

SERVES 8

2 eggs

75g/3oz/6 tbsp caster (superfine) sugar

grated rind of 1 lemon

50g/2oz/½ cup sifted plain (all-purpose) flour

shredded lemon rind, to decorate

For the filling

2 eggs, separated

75g/3oz/6 tbsp caster (superfine) sugar

grated rind and juice of 1 lemon

30ml/2 tbsp water

15ml/1 tbsp powdered gelatine

120ml/4fl oz/½ cup low-fat fromage frais or low-fat cream cheese

For the icing

15ml/1 tbsp lemon juice

115g/4oz/1 cup icing (confectioners') sugar, sifted

Nutritional information	
Calories	202kcals/849kJ
Fat	2.81g
Saturated fat	0.79g
Cholesterol	96.4mg
Fibre	0.2g

Variations

• Instead of lemon rind, try using a lime for a slightly different citrus flavour.

• If you don't want to make icing, simply dust the top of the cake with icing (confectioners') sugar.

Cook's Tip

The lemon mousse should be just setting when the egg whites are added. You can speed up this process by placing the bowl of mousse in a larger bowl of iced water.

1 Preheat the oven to 180°C/350°F/ Gas 4. Grease and line a 20cm/8in loose-bottomed cake tin (pan). Whisk the eggs, sugar and lemon rind together with a hand-held electric whisk until thick and mousse-like. Gently fold in the flour, then turn the mixture into the prepared tin.

2 Bake for 20–25 minutes until the cake springs back when lightly pressed in the centre. Turn on to a wire rack to cool. Once cold, split the cake in half horizontally and return the lower half to the clean cake tin.

3 Make the filling. Put the egg yolks, sugar, lemon rind and juice into a grease-free bowl. Beat with an electric whisk until thick, pale and creamy.

4 Pour the water into a heatproof bowl and sprinkle the gelatine on top. Leave until spongy, then stir over simmering water until dissolved. Cool, then whisk into the yolk mixture. Fold in the fromage frais or cream cheese. When the mixture begins to set, whisk the egg whites to soft peaks. Fold the egg whites into the mousse mixture.

5 Pour the lemon mousse over the sponge in the cake tin, spreading it to the edges. Set the second layer of sponge on top and chill until set.

6 Slide a spatula between the tin and the cake. Transfer to a plate. For the icing, add lemon juice to the icing sugar to make a thick mixture that will coat a wooden spoon. Spread the icing over the cake. Decorate with lemon shreds.

MUFFINS

Served warm from the oven, these bitesize cakes are a pleasure
for the palate – and you can enjoy them without feeling
too guilty. Although they look and taste divine, these
muffins are all low in fat.

Blueberry Muffins

Warm muffins with a hint of vanilla are an old favourite – and they are not high in calories or in fat.

MAKES 12

150g/5oz/1¼ cups plain (all-purpose) flour
50g/2oz/¼ cup sugar
10ml/2 tsp baking powder
2.5ml/½ tsp salt
2 eggs
60ml/4 tbsp butter, melted
175ml/6fl oz/¾ cup skimmed milk
5ml/1 tsp vanilla extract
5ml/1 tsp grated lemon rind
115g/4oz/1 cup fresh blueberries

Nutritional information

Calories	124kcals/524kJ
Fat	3.9g
Saturated fat	0.8g
Cholesterol	33mg
Fibre	0.8g

1 Preheat the oven to 200°C/400°F/ Gas 6.

2 Grease a 12-cup muffin tin (pan) or use paper cases.

3 Sift the flour, sugar, baking powder and salt into a bowl.

4 In another bowl, whisk the eggs until blended. Add the melted butter, milk, vanilla extract and lemon rind, and stir to combine. Make a well in the dry ingredients and pour in the egg mixture. With a large metal spoon, stir just until the flour is moistened, not until the mixture is smooth.

5 Fold in the blueberries using the large metal spoon.

6 Spoon the batter into the cups, leaving room for the muffins to rise. Bake for 20–25 minutes, or until risen and golden brown. Cool in the tin for about 5 minutes before turning out.

Apple Cranberry Muffins

Fruit and nuts with a touch of spice are a winning combination in these mouthwatering muffins.

1 Preheat the oven to 180°C/350°F/
Gas 4. Grease a 12-cup muffin tin
(pan) or use paper cases.

2 Melt the butter or margarine over
gentle heat. Set aside to cool.

3 Place the egg in a mixing bowl and
whisk lightly. Add the melted butter
or margarine and whisk to combine.

4 Add the sugar, orange rind and
juice. Whisk to blend, then set
aside. In a large bowl, sift together the
flour, baking powder, bicarbonate of
soda, cinnamon, nutmeg, allspice,
ginger and salt. Set aside.

5 Quarter, core and peel the
apples. Then, dice them coarsely,
using a sharp knife.

Nutritional information

Calories	175kcals/733kJ
Fat	9.1g
Saturated fat	1.4g
Cholesterol	16mg
Fibre	1.4g

6 Make a well in the dry ingredients
and pour in the egg mixture. Using
a large metal spoon, stir until just
blended. Add the apples, cranberries and
walnuts and stir to blend.

7 Fill the muffin cups three-quarters
full and bake for 25–30 minutes,
or until well risen and firm in the middle.
Transfer the muffins to a rack to cool.
Dust lightly with icing sugar before
serving, if you wish.

MAKES 12
60ml/4 tbsp butter or margarine
1 egg
175g/6oz/scant 1 cup sugar
grated rind of 1 large orange
120ml/4fl oz/½ cup orange juice
175g/6oz/1½ cups plain
    (all-purpose) flour
2.5ml/½ tsp baking powder
2.5ml/½ tsp bicarbonate of soda
    (baking soda)
5ml/1 tsp ground cinnamon
2.5ml/½ tsp freshly grated nutmeg
2.5ml/½ tsp ground allspice
1.5ml/¼ tsp ground ginger
1.5ml/¼ tsp salt
1–2 eating apples
115g/4oz/1 cup cranberries
50g/2oz/½ cup chopped walnuts
icing (confectioners') sugar,
    for dusting (optional)

Raspberry Muffins

These American muffins are made using baking powder and low-fat buttermilk, giving them a light and spongy texture. They are delicious to eat at any time of the day.

MAKES 10–12

275g/10oz/2½ cups plain
   (all-purpose) flour
15ml/1 tbsp baking powder
115g/4oz/generous ½ cup caster
   (superfine) sugar
1 egg
250ml/8fl oz/1 cup buttermilk
60ml/4 tbsp sunflower oil
150g/5oz/scant 1 cup raspberries

Nutritional information	
Calories	171kcals/719kJ
Fat	4.55g
Saturated fat	0.71g
Cholesterol	16.5mg
Fibre	1.02g

1 Preheat the oven to 200°C/400°F/ Gas 6. Grease a 12-cup muffin tin (pan) or use paper cases. Sift the flour and baking powder into a mixing bowl, stir in the sugar, then make a well in the centre.

2 Mix the egg, buttermilk and sunflower oil in a bowl, pour into the flour mixture and mix quickly.

3 Add the raspberries and lightly fold in with a metal spoon. Spoon the mixture into the tin or paper cases.

4 Bake the muffins for 20–25 minutes until golden brown and firm in the middle. Cool on a wire rack and serve.

Spiced Banana Muffins

These light and nutritious muffins include banana for added fibre, and make a tasty tea-time treat. If you like, slice off the tops and fill with jam.

1 Preheat the oven to 200°C/400°F/ Gas 6. Grease a 12-cup muffin tin (pan) or use paper cases. Sift together both flours, the baking powder, salt and mixed spice into a bowl, then put the bran remaining in the sieve (strainer) into the bowl. Stir in the sugar.

2 Melt the margarine and pour it into a mixing bowl. Cool slightly, then beat in the egg, milk and grated orange rind.

3 Using a large metal spoon, gently fold in the dry ingredients. Mash the banana with a fork, then stir it gently into the mixture, being careful not to overmix.

4 Spoon the mixture into the tin or paper cases. Combine the oats and hazelnuts and sprinkle a little of the mixture over each muffin.

5 Bake in the preheated oven for 20 minutes until the muffins are well risen and golden, and a skewer inserted in the centre comes out clean. Transfer to a wire rack and allow to cool. These muffins can be served warm or cold.

MAKES 12

75g/3oz/²⁄₃ cup plain (all-purpose) wholemeal (whole-wheat) flour
50g/2oz/½ cup plain (all-purpose) white flour
10ml/2 tsp baking powder
a pinch of salt
5ml/1 tsp mixed (apple pie) spice
40g/1½oz/3 tbsp soft light brown sugar
50g/2oz/¼ cup polyunsaturated margarine
1 egg, beaten
150ml/¼ pint/²⁄₃ cup semi-skimmed (low-fat) milk
grated rind of 1 orange
1 ripe banana
20g/¾oz/¼ cup rolled oats
20g/¾oz/scant ¼ cup chopped hazelnuts

Nutritional information	
Calories	139kcals/582kJ
Fat	5g
Saturated fat	1g
Cholesterol	0mg
Fibre	0.13g

Carrot Muffins

These moist and flavourful muffins, with a little kick of spice, are sure to be a favourite at tea time.

MAKES 12

175g/6oz/¾ cup margarine, at room
    temperature
75g/3oz/scant ½ cup soft dark brown sugar
1 egg
15ml/1 tbsp water
150g/5oz/2 cups grated carrots
150g/5oz/1¼ cups plain (all-purpose) flour
5ml/1 tsp baking powder
2.5ml/½ tsp bicarbonate of soda (baking soda)
5ml/1 tsp ground cinnamon
1.5ml/¼ tsp freshly grated nutmeg
2.5ml/½ tsp salt

Nutritional information

Calories	155kcals/647kJ
Fat	9.2g
Saturated fat	1.8g
Cholesterol	13mg
Fibre	0.8g

1 Preheat the oven to 180°C/350°F/
Gas 4. Grease a 12-cup muffin tin
(pan) or use paper cases.

2 With an electric mixer, cream the
margarine and sugar until they are
light and fluffy. Beat in the egg and
water. Stir in the carrots.

3 Sift over the flour, baking powder,
bicarbonate of soda, cinnamon,
nutmeg and salt. Stir to blend.

4 Spoon the batter into the prepared
muffin cups, filling them almost
to the top. Bake for about 35 minutes,
until risen and firm in the middle.
Leave to stand for 10 minutes, then
transfer to a rack.

Variation

Mix 60g/2¼oz/generous 4 tbsp low-fat
soft cheese with 45ml/3 tbsp reduced-fat
fromage frais. Add 5ml/1 tsp grated orange
rind, mix and spread over the muffins.

Dried Cherry Muffins

Muffins make a wonderful breakfast, particularly on special occasions.

1 In a mixing bowl, combine the yogurt and cherries. Cover and leave to stand for 30 minutes. Preheat the oven to 180°C/350°F/Gas 4. Grease a 16-cup muffin tin (pan) or use paper cases.

2 With an electric mixer, cream the butter and sugar together until they are light and fluffy.

3 Add the eggs, one at a time, beating well after each addition.

4 Add the vanilla extract and the cherry mixture, and stir to blend. Set aside. In another bowl, sift together the flour, baking powder, bicarbonate of soda and salt. Fold into the cherry mixture in three batches; do not overmix.

5 Fill the prepared muffin cups two-thirds full. For even baking, half-fill any empty cups with water. Bake for about 20 minutes, or until well risen and firm in the middle. Transfer to a rack.

MAKES 16

225g/8oz/1 cup natural (plain) yogurt
225g/8oz/1 cup dried cherries
115g/4oz/½ cup butter
175g/6oz/scant 1 cup caster (superfine) sugar
2 eggs
5ml/1 tsp vanilla extract
200g/7oz/1⅔ cups plain (all-purpose) flour
30ml/2 tbsp baking powder
5ml/1 tsp bicarbonate of soda (baking soda)
0.75ml/⅛ tsp salt

Nutritional information

Calories	197kcals/826kJ
Fat	6.8g
Saturated fat	1.4g
Cholesterol	25mg
Fibre	0.7g

Oatmeal Buttermilk Muffins

These easy-to-make muffins make a healthy treat at breakfast or any time of the day.

2 Grease a 12-cup muffin tin (pan) or use paper cases.

MAKES 12

75g/3oz/scant 1 cup rolled oats
250ml/8fl oz/1 cup buttermilk
115g/4oz/½ cup butter
75g/3oz/scant ½ cup soft dark brown sugar
1 egg
115g/4oz/1 cup plain (all-purpose) flour
5ml/1 tsp baking powder
2.5ml/½ tsp salt
25g/1oz/¼ cup raisins

3 Preheat the oven to 200°C/400°F/ Gas 6. Using an electric mixer, cream the butter and sugar until light and fluffy. Beat in the egg.

4 In another bowl, sift together the flour, baking powder and salt. Stir the dry ingredients into the butter mixture, alternating with the oat mixture. Fold in the raisins, taking care not to overmix.

Nutritional information	
Calories	213kcals/893kJ
Fat	9.3g
Saturated fat	1.9g
Cholesterol	17mg
Fibre	1.2g

1 In a bowl, combine the oats and buttermilk and leave to soak for 1 hour.

5 Fill the prepared cups two-thirds full. Bake for about 20–25 minutes, until a cake tester or skewer inserted in the centre comes out clean. Transfer to a wire rack to cool.

Pumpkin Muffins

Pumpkin has a mild, sweet flavour and makes a delicious, moist muffin.

MAKES 14

115g/4oz/½ cup butter or margarine
165g/5½oz/⅔ cup soft dark brown sugar
150ml/¼ pint/⅔ cup molasses
1 egg, beaten
225g/8oz/1 cup cooked or canned pumpkin
200g/7oz/1⅔ cups plain (all-purpose) flour
1.5ml/¼ tsp salt
5ml/1 tsp bicarbonate of soda (baking soda)
7.5ml/1½ tsp ground cinnamon
5ml/1 tsp freshly grated nutmeg
25g/1oz/2 tbsp currants or raisins

Nutritional information	
Calories	196kcals/821kJ
Fat	7.3g
Saturated fat	1.4g
Cholesterol	14mg
Fibre	0.8g

1 Preheat the oven to 200°C/400°F/ Gas 6. Grease a 14-cup muffin tin (pan) or use paper cases. Cream the butter or margarine until soft.

2 Add the sugar and molasses and beat the mixture until light and fluffy. Add the egg and pumpkin and stir together to thoroughly combine. Sift over the flour, salt, bicarbonate of soda, cinnamon and nutmeg. Fold to blend; do not overmix.

3 Fold in the currants or raisins. Spoon the batter into the prepared muffin cups, filling them three-quarters full.

4 Bake for about 12–15 minutes, until well risen and firm in the middle. Transfer to a rack. Serve warm or cold.

Raisin Bran Muffins

High in fibre and also high in flavour, these muffins are a perfect tea time treat.

MAKES 15

60ml/4 tbsp butter or margarine
75g/3oz/²⁄₃ cup plain (all-purpose) white flour
50g/2oz/½ cup plain (all-purpose) wholemeal (whole-wheat) flour
7.5ml/1½ tsp bicarbonate of soda (baking soda)
0.75ml/⅛ tsp salt
5ml/1 tsp ground cinnamon
40g/1½oz/½ cup bran
75g/3oz/generous ½ cup raisins
50g/2oz/¼ cup soft dark brown sugar
50g/2oz/¼ cup granulated (white) sugar
1 egg, beaten
250ml/8fl oz/1 cup buttermilk
juice of ½ lemon

Nutritional information

Calories	131kcals/551kJ
Fat	4.1g
Saturated fat	0.9g
Cholesterol	13mg
Fibre	1.7g

Cook's Tips

• To ensure that the muffins cook evenly, half-fill any unused cups in the muffin tin (pan) with water.
• Serve these muffins warm or at room temperature, either on their own, or with low-fat cream cheese.
• If buttermilk is not available, add 10ml/2 tsp lemon juice or vinegar to the equivalent amount of milk. Leave the mixture to stand and curdle for about 30 minutes, then use to prepare the muffin batter.
• Bran is made from the outer layer of cereal, such as the husks of wheat or oats. It is a natural product that is valued for its fibre content; it also adds texture and flavour to the muffins.

Variation

You could try other mild and sweet spices in these muffins instead of cinnamon. Mixed (apple pie) spice will be just as good in this recipe.

1 Preheat the oven to 200°C/400°F/ Gas 6. Lightly grease a 15-cup muffin tin (pan) or use paper cases to line the muffin tin.

2 Place the butter or margarine in a heavy pan and melt over a gentle heat. Set aside.

3 In a mixing bowl, sift together the white flour, wholemeal flour, bicarbonate of soda, salt and cinnamon.

4 Add the bran, raisins and sugars and stir until blended.

5 In another bowl, mix together the egg, buttermilk, lemon juice and melted butter or margarine.

6 Add the buttermilk mixture to the dry ingredients. Stir lightly and quickly until just moistened; do not mix until smooth as this will ruin the texture.

7 Spoon the batter into the prepared muffin cups or paper cases, filling them almost to the top. Half-fill any empty cups with water before placing in the oven.

8 Bake until golden, for 15–20 minutes. Leave to stand for about 5 minutes, before transferring to a wire rack to cool. Serve warm or at room temperature. Store in an airtight container for up to 3 days.

Prune Muffins

All types of fruit can be used as a delicious addition to muffins – prunes are a healthy option.

MAKES 12

1 egg

250ml/8fl oz/1 cup skimmed milk

50ml/2fl oz/¼ cup vegetable oil

50g/2oz/¼ cup granulated (white) sugar

30ml/2 tbsp soft dark brown sugar

225g/8oz/2 cups plain
   (all-purpose) flour

30ml/2 tsp baking powder

2.5ml/½ tsp salt

1.5ml/¼ tsp freshly grated nutmeg

150g/5oz/¾ cup cooked pitted
   prunes, chopped

Nutritional information

Calories	177kcals/745kJ
Fat	4.66g
Saturated fat	0.6g
Cholesterol	16mg
Fibre	1.5g

1 Preheat the oven to 200°C/400°F/ Gas 6. Grease a 12-cup muffin tin (pan) or use paper cases.

2 Break the egg into a mixing bowl and beat with a whisk or fork. Beat in the milk and oil.

3 Stir in the granulated sugar and the dark brown sugar. Set aside.

4 Sift the flour, baking powder, salt and nutmeg into a mixing bowl. Add the egg and stir. The batter should be slightly lumpy.

5 Fold in the prunes with a spatula or a large spoon.

6 Fill the prepared cups two-thirds full. Bake until golden brown, or for about 20 minutes. Leave to stand for 10 minutes before turning out. Allow to cool slightly, then serve warm or at room temperature.

Cook's Tips

• Prunes are full of fibre and have long been known as a natural laxative.
• Store the muffins in an airtight container for up to 3 days.
• Soak the prunes for a few hours before simmering in enough water to cover. They will take about 20 minutes to cook. Remove the pits from the cooked fruit before using.
• For extra flavour, cook the prunes with lemon juice, lemon rind and a sprinkling of mixed (apple pie) spice.

Yogurt Honey Muffins

Serve with low-fat yogurt and a drizzle of honey for a delicious treat.

1 Preheat the oven to 190°C/375°F/ Gas 5. Grease a 12-cup muffin tin (pan) or use paper cases.

2 Melt the butter and honey together in a small pan, over a gentle heat. Stir to combine. Remove from the heat and set aside to cool slightly.

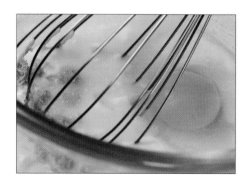

3 In a bowl, whisk together the yogurt, egg, lemon rind and juice.

4 In another bowl, sift together the dry ingredients: the plain flour, wholemeal flour, bicarbonate of soda and the grated nutmeg.

5 Stir the butter and honey into the yogurt mixture, then fold in the dry ingredients until just blended.

6 Fill the prepared cups two-thirds full. Bake until the tops spring back when touched lightly, This should take around 20–25 minutes. The muffins will be well risen and firm in the middle.

7 Leave the muffins to cool in the tin for 5 minutes before turning out of the cups. Serve them warm or at room temperature.

Variation

There is a wide range of honeys available, with various flavours. They will give a subtly different taste to the muffins, so it is worth experimenting with a few varieties to see which you prefer.

MAKES 12

60ml/4 tbsp butter
75ml/5 tbsp clear honey
225g/8oz/1 cup natural (plain) yogurt
1 large (US extra large) egg
grated rind of 1 lemon
50ml/2fl oz/¼ cup lemon juice
115g/4oz/1 cup plain (all-purpose) flour
115g/4oz/1 cup plain (all-purpose)
    wholemeal (whole-wheat) flour
7.5ml/1½ tsp bicarbonate of soda (baking soda)
0.75ml/⅛ tsp freshly grated nutmeg

Nutritional information	
Calories	131kcals/551kJ
Fat	4.1g
Saturated fat	0.9g
Cholesterol	13mg
Fibre	1.7g

Blackberry and Rose Water Muffins

Bring a taste of the countryside to coffee time with tantalizing hedgerow fruits and delicate rose water.

MAKES 12

300g/11oz/2⅔ cups plain
(all-purpose) flour
50g/2oz/generous ¼ cup soft light
brown sugar
60ml/4 tsp baking powder
a pinch of salt
60g/2¼oz/generous ½ cup chopped
blanched almonds
90g/3½oz/generous 1 cup
fresh blackberries
2 eggs
200ml/7fl oz/scant 1 cup milk
60ml/4 tbsp melted butter
15ml/1 tbsp sloe gin
15ml/1 tbsp rose water

1 Preheat the oven to 200°C/400°F/
Gas 6. Grease a 12-cup muffin tin
(pan) or use paper cases. Mix the flour,
sugar, baking powder and salt in a bowl.
Add the almonds and blackberries, mixing
well to coat with the flour mixture.

2 In another bowl, mix the eggs with
the milk, then gradually add the
butter, sloe gin and rose water. Make a
well in the centre of the bowl of dry
ingredients and add the egg and milk
mixture. Stir well.

3 Spoon the mixture into the greased
muffin tin or paper cases. Bake for
20–25 minutes or until browned. Turn
out the muffins on to a wire rack to
cool. Serve with butter.

Cook's Tip

Sloe gin is made from sloes, the fruit of
the blackthorn, which is related to the
plum. The sloes are packed into jars with
sugar and covered with gin, then left a
few weeks to mature.

Nutritional information

Calories	194kcals/813kJ
Fat	8.1g
Saturated fat	1.32g
Cholesterol	32.8mg
Fibre	1.4g

Date and Apple Muffins

You will only need one or two of these wholesome muffins per person, as they are very filling.

1 Preheat the oven to 200°C/400°F/ Gas 6. Grease a 12-cup muffin tin (pan) or use paper cases. Put the wholemeal flour in a mixing bowl. Sift in the white flour with the cinnamon and baking powder. Rub in the margarine until the mixture resembles breadcrumbs, then stir in the muscovado sugar.

2 Quarter and core the apple, chop the flesh finely and set aside. Stir a little of the apple juice with the pear and apple spread until smooth. Mix in the remaining juice, then add to the rubbed-in dry ingredients with the egg. Add the chopped apple to the bowl with the dates. Stir quickly until just combined.

3 Divide the mixture evenly among the muffin cases.

4 Sprinkle with the chopped pecan nuts. Bake the muffins for 20–25 minutes until golden brown and firm in the middle. Transfer to a wire rack and serve while still warm.

Variation

Use a pear in place of the eating apple and chopped ready-to-eat dried apricots in place of the dates. Mixed (apple pie) spice is a good alternative to cinnamon.

MAKES 12

150g/5oz/1¼ cups self-raising (self-rising) wholemeal (whole-wheat) flour
150g/5oz/1¼ cups self-raising (self-rising) white flour
5ml/1 tsp ground cinnamon
5ml/1 tsp baking powder
25g/1oz/2 tbsp soft margarine
75g/3oz/scant ½ cup light muscovado (brown) sugar
1 eating apple
250ml/8fl oz/1 cup apple juice
30ml/2 tbsp pear and apple spread
1 egg, lightly beaten
75g/3oz/½ cup chopped dates
15ml/1 tbsp chopped pecan nuts

Nutritional information	
Calories	163kcal/686kJ
Fat	2.98g
Saturated fat	0.47g
Cholesterol	16.04mg
Fibre	1.97g

Cherry Marmalade Muffins

Serve fresh from the oven with marmalade, for a filling, tasty breakfast.

MAKES 12

225g/8oz/2 cups self-raising (self-rising) flour
5ml/1 tsp mixed (apple pie) spice
75g/3oz/6 tbsp caster (superfine) sugar
115g/4oz/½ cup glacé (candied)
    cherries, quartered
30ml/2 tbsp orange marmalade
150ml/¼ pint/⅔ cup skimmed milk
50g/2oz/¼ cup soft sunflower margarine
marmalade, to brush

Nutritional information	
Calories	154kcals/650kJ
Fat	3.66g
Saturated fat	0.68g
Cholesterol	0.54mg
Fibre	0.69g

1 Preheat the oven to 200°C/400°F/ Gas 6. Lightly grease a 12-cup muffin tin (pan) or use paper cases.

2 Sift together the flour and spice, then stir in the sugar and cherries.

3 Mix the marmalade with the milk and beat into the dry ingredients with the margarine. Spoon into the greased tin. Bake for 20–25 minutes, until the muffins are golden brown and firm in the middle.

4 Turn out on to a wire rack and brush the tops with warmed marmalade. Serve warm or cold. Store in an airtight container for up to 3 days.

Variation

To make honey, nut and lemon muffins, substitute 30ml/2 tbsp clear honey for the orange marmalade. Instead of the glacé cherries, use 50g/2oz toasted chopped hazelnuts. Add the juice and finely grated rind of one lemon.

Fruit Salad Slices

Try these delicious fruit salad slices as an alternative to a traditional fruit cake.

1 Soak the dried fruits in the tea for several hours, or overnight. Drain and reserve the liquid.

2 Preheat the oven to 180°C/350°F/ Gas 4. Grease an 18cm/7in round cake tin (pan) and line the base with baking parchment.

3 Sift the flour into a bowl with the nutmeg. Stir in the muscovado sugar, fruit and tea. Add the oil and milk and mix well.

You can use any combination of dried fruits that you have to hand, in this rich cake. Cherries, raisins, currants, sultanas (golden raisins) and dates would be a good combination to use instead of the dried fruit salad mixture.

4 Spoon the mixture into the prepared tin and sprinkle the top with demerara sugar. Bake for 50–55 minutes or until firm. Turn the cake out and leave to cool on a wire rack. Cut into slices. Store in an airtight container for up to 3 days.

SERVES 8

175g/6oz/1 cup roughly chopped dried fruit salad mixture, such as apples, apricots, prunes and peaches
250ml/8fl oz/1 cup hot black tea
225g/8oz/2 cups self-raising (self-rising) wholemeal (whole-wheat) flour
5ml/1 tsp freshly grated nutmeg
50g/2oz/4 tbsp muscovado (molasses) sugar
45ml/3 tbsp sunflower oil
45ml/3 tbsp skimmed milk
demerara (raw) sugar, to sprinkle

Nutritional information	
Calories	201kcals/848kJ
Fat	4.99g
Saturated fat	0.65g
Cholesterol	0.1mg
Fibre	3.89g

SCONES, BUNS and COOKIES

Tea time will never be the same again once you have tried these recipes. They are also a delicious treat to add to lunch boxes – and because they are low in fat, they are a healthier option for children as well as adults.

Pineapple Drop Scones

Making the batter with pineapple juice instead of milk cuts down on fat and adds an interesting flavour.

2 Add the egg with half the pineapple juice and gradually incorporate the surrounding flour to make a smooth batter. Beat in the remaining juice with the chopped pineapple.

3 Lightly oil the griddle or pan. Drop tablespoons of the batter on to the surface, leaving them until they bubble and the bubbles begin to burst.

MAKES 24

115g/4oz/1 cup self-raising (self-rising) wholemeal (whole-wheat) flour
115g/4oz/1 cup self-raising (self-rising) white flour
5ml/1 tsp ground cinnamon
15ml/1 tbsp caster (superfine) sugar
1 egg, beaten
300ml/½ pint/1¼ cups pineapple juice
75g/3oz/½ cup semi-dried pineapple, chopped
vegetable oil, for greasing

 1 Preheat a griddle (grill) pan, heavy frying pan or an electric frying pan. Put the wholemeal flour in a large mixing bowl. Sift in the white flour, add the cinnamon and sugar and make a well in the centre.

4 Turn the drop scones with a palette knife or metal spatula and cook until the underside is golden brown. Keep the cooked scones warm and moist by wrapping them in a clean napkin while continuing to cook successive batches.

Nutritional information	
Calories	51kcals/215kJ
Fat	0.81g
Saturated fat	0.14g
Cholesterol	8.02mg
Fibre	0.76g

Drop Scones

These little scones are quick and easy to make on a griddle, and contain very little fat.

MAKES 18

225g/8oz/2 cups self-raising (self-rising) flour
2.5ml/½ tsp salt
15ml/1 tbsp caster (superfine) sugar
1 egg, beaten
300ml/½ pint/1¼ cups skimmed milk
vegetable oil, for greasing

1 Preheat a griddle (grill) pan, frying pan or an electric frying pan. Sift the flour and salt into a mixing bowl. Stir in the sugar and make a well in the centre.

4 Turn the drop scones over with a palette knife or metal spatula and cook until the underside is golden brown. Keep the cooked drop scones warm and moist by wrapping them in a clean napkin while cooking successive batches.

Nutritional information

Calories	64kcals/270kJ
Fat	1.09g
Saturated fat	0.2g
Cholesterol	11.4mg
Fibre	0.43g

2 Add the egg and half the milk, then gradually incorporate the flour to make a smooth batter. Beat in the remaining milk.

3 Lightly oil the griddle or pan. Drop tablespoons of the batter on to the surface, leaving them until they bubble and the bubbles begin to burst.

Variation

For savoury scones, omit the sugar and add 2 finely chopped spring onions (scallions) and 15ml/1 tbsp freshly grated Parmesan cheese.

Wholemeal Scones

Made with a mixture of flours, these scones are a high fibre, healthy alternative.

MAKES 16

175g/6oz/¾ cup cold butter

225g/8oz/2 cups plain (all-purpose)
   wholemeal (whole-wheat) flour

175g/6oz/1½ cups plain (all-purpose)
   white flour

30ml/2 tbsp caster (superfine) sugar

2.5ml/½ tsp salt

12.5ml/2½ tsp bicarbonate of soda

2 eggs

175ml/6fl oz/¾ cup buttermilk

25g/1oz/¼ cup raisins

Nutritional information

Calories	197kcals/826kJ
Fat	9.8g
Saturated fat	2g
Cholesterol	25mg
Fibre	2g

1 Preheat the oven to 200°C/400°F/ Gas 6. Grease and flour a baking sheet.

2 Cut the butter into small pieces before mixing with the flour.

3 Combine the dry ingredients in a bowl. Add the butter and rub in with your fingertips until the mixture resembles coarse crumbs. Set aside.

4 In another bowl, whisk together the eggs and buttermilk. Set aside 30ml/2 tbsp for glazing.

5 Stir the remaining egg mixture into the dry ingredients until it just holds together. Stir in the raisins.

6 Roll out the dough about 2cm/¾in thick. Stamp out rounds with a cutter. Place on the prepared sheet and brush with the reserved glaze.

7 Bake in the preheated oven for 12–15 minutes, until golden. Allow to cool slightly before serving.

Orange Raisin Scones

A little grated orange rind adds an extra-special piquancy to these delicious scones.

1 Preheat the oven to 220°C/425°F/
Gas 7. Grease and flour a large
baking sheet.

2 Combine the dry ingredients in a
large bowl. Add the butter and
margarine and rub in with your
fingertips until the mixture resembles
coarse crumbs.

MAKES 16

225g/8oz/2 cups plain (all-purpose) flour
25ml/1½ tbsp baking powder
75g/3oz/6 tbsp caster (superfine) sugar
2.5ml/½ tsp salt
75ml/5 tbsp butter, diced
75ml/5 tbsp margarine, diced
grated rind of 1 large orange
50g/2oz/⅓ cup raisins
120g/4fl oz/½ cup buttermilk
milk, for glazing

5 Place on the prepared sheet and
brush the tops of the scones with
milk. Bake for about 12–15 minutes, until
golden. Serve hot or warm with low-fat
crème fraîche and low-sugar jam.

Nutritional information

Calories	164kcals/687kJ
Fat	7.9g
Saturated fat	1.6g
Cholesterol	1mg
Fibre	0.7g

3 Add the orange rind and raisins.
Gradually stir in the buttermilk
to form a soft dough.

4 Roll out the dough about 2cm/¾in
thick. Stamp out rounds with a cutter.

Cook's Tip

For light, tender scones, handle the dough
as little as possible. If you wish, split the
scones when cool and toast them under a
preheated grill (broiler). Butter and eat
them while still hot.

Sunflower Scones

Add a bit of crunch to your scones with this combination of sunflower seeds and sultanas.

MAKES 10–12

225g/8oz/2 cups self-raising
   (self-rising) flour
5ml/1 tsp baking powder
25g/1oz/2 tbsp soft sunflower margarine
25g/1oz/2 tbsp caster (superfine) sugar
50g/2oz/⅓ cup sultanas (golden raisins)
30ml/2 tbsp sunflower seeds
150g/5oz/⅔ cup natural (plain) yogurt
about 30–45ml/2–3 tbsp skimmed milk

Nutritional information	
Calories	176kcals/742kJ
Fat	5.32g
Saturated fat	0.81g
Cholesterol	0.84mg
Fibre	1.26g

1 Preheat the oven to 230°C/450°F/ Gas 8. Lightly oil a baking sheet. Sift the flour and baking powder into a bowl and rub in the margarine evenly.

2 Stir in the sugar, sultanas and half the sunflower seeds, then mix in the yogurt, with just enough milk to make a fairly soft, but not sticky, dough.

3 Roll out the dough on a lightly floured surface to about 2cm/¾in thick. Cut into 6cm/2½in flower shapes or rounds with a pastry (cookie) cutter and lift on to the baking sheet.

4 Brush with milk and sprinkle with the reserved sunflower seeds, then bake for 10–12 minutes, until well risen and golden brown.

5 Cool the scones on a wire rack. Serve split and spread with jam or low-fat spread.

Cook's Tip

Sunflower seeds are often eaten as a healthy snack; they are a good source of fibre, protein, vitamins and minerals, such as potassium, magnesium, iron, phosphorus, selenium, calcium and zinc. They are also rich in cholesterol-lowering phytosterols and contain very little sugar. However, because they have a high fat content, they do not store well for long periods. Don't buy too many sunflower seeds at a time, and source them from a store that has a quick turnover, so you can ensure they are fresh.

Prune and Peel Rock Buns

Split these buns and serve with fromage frais or ricotta cheese, if you like.

MAKES 12

225g/8oz/2 cups plain (all-purpose) flour
10ml/2 tsp baking powder
75g/3oz/⅓ cup demerara (raw) sugar
50g/2oz/¼ cup chopped
    ready-to-eat prunes
50g/2oz/⅓ cup chopped mixed peel
finely grated rind of 1 lemon
50ml/2fl oz/¼ cup sunflower oil
75ml/5 tbsp skimmed milk

1 Preheat the oven to 200°C/400°F/
Gas 6. Lightly oil a large baking
sheet. Sift together the flour and baking
powder, then stir in the sugar, prunes,
peel and lemon rind.

2 Mix the oil and milk, then stir into
the mixture, to make a dough that
just binds together.

3 Spoon into heaps on the baking
sheet and bake for 20 minutes. Cool.

Variation

Try substituting other dried fruits
instead of the prunes, such as apricots
or cranberries.

Nutritional information	
Calories	135kcals/570kJ
Fat	3.35g
Saturated fat	0.44g
Cholesterol	0.13mg
Fibre	0.86g

Banana and Apricot Chelsea Buns

These old favourites are given a low-fat twist and a delectable fruit filling.

SERVES 9

about 90ml/6 tbsp warm skimmed milk

5ml/1 tsp dried yeast

a pinch of sugar

225g/8oz/2 cups strong white
    bread flour

10ml/2 tsp mixed (apple pie) spice

2.5ml/½ tsp salt

50g/2oz/¼ cup caster (superfine) sugar

25g/1oz/2 tbsp soft margarine

1 egg, beaten

For the filling

1 large ripe banana

175g/6oz/1 cup ready-to-eat
    dried apricots

30ml/2 tbsp caster (superfine) sugar

30ml/2 tbsp light muscovado
    (brown) sugar

For the glaze

30ml/2 tbsp caster (superfine) sugar

30ml/2 tbsp water

Nutritional information	
Calories	214kcals/901kJ
Fat	2.18g
Saturated fat	0.63g
Cholesterol	21.59mg
Fibre	2.18g

1 Lightly grease an 18cm/7in square cake tin (pan). Put the warm milk in a jug (pitcher) and sprinkle the yeast on top. Add a pinch of sugar to help activate the yeast, mix well and leave for 30 minutes.

2 Sift the flour, spice and salt into a mixing bowl. Stir in the caster sugar, rub in the margarine, then stir in the yeast mixture and the egg. Gradually mix together to make a soft dough, adding extra milk if needed.

3 Turn out the dough on to a floured surface and knead for 5 minutes until smooth and elastic. Return the dough to the clean bowl, cover with a damp dish towel and leave in a warm place for about 2 hours, until doubled in bulk.

4 To prepare the filling, mash the banana in a bowl. Using scissors, snip the apricots into pieces, then stir into the banana with the sugars.

Brush the buns with the glaze while they are still hot. Do not leave the buns in the tin for too long or the glaze will stick to the sides, making them very difficult to remove.

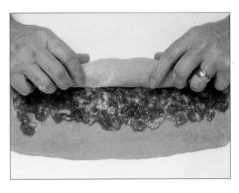

5 Knead the dough on a floured surface for 2 minutes, then roll out to a 30 x 23cm/12 x 9in rectangle. Spread the banana and apricot filling over the dough and roll up lengthways like a Swiss (jelly) roll, making sure the join is underneath.

6 Cut into nine equal pieces. Place, cut side down, in the tin, cover and leave to rise for 30 minutes. Preheat the oven to 200°C/ 400°F/Gas 6 and bake for 20–25 minutes until they are golden brown. Mix the caster sugar and water in a pan. Heat gently until dissolved, then boil for 2 minutes. Brush the cooked buns with the glaze.

Blueberry Streusel Slice

The soft berry filling is a wonderful contrast to the crunchy nutty topping.

MAKES ABOUT 30 SLICES

225g/8oz shortcrust pastry, thawed if frozen
50g/2oz/½ cup plain (all-purpose) flour
1.5ml/¼ tsp baking powder
40g/1½oz/3 tbsp butter or margarine
50g/2oz/¼ cup soft light brown sugar
25g/1oz/½ cup fresh white breadcrumbs
1.5ml/¼ tsp salt
50g/2oz/½ cup flaked (sliced) or
    chopped almonds
30ml/4 tbsp blackberry jelly
115g/4oz/1 cup blueberries

Nutritional information

Calories	77kcals/322kJ
Fat	4.16g
Saturated fat	1.57g
Cholesterol	5.84mg
Fibre	0.95g

1 Preheat the oven to 180°F/350°F/
Gas 4. Roll out the pastry on a lightly
floured surface to line an 18 x 28cm/
7 x 11in Swiss roll tin (jelly roll pan).
Prick the base evenly with a fork.

2 Rub together the flour, baking
powder, butter or margarine, sugar,
breadcrumbs and salt until crumbly,
then mix in the almonds.

3 Spread the pastry with the jelly,
sprinkle with the blueberries,
then cover evenly with the almond
mixture, pressing down lightly.
Bake for 20 minutes, then reduce
the temperature to 160°C/325°F/Gas 3
and cook for a further 10–20 minutes.

4 Remove from the oven when golden
on the top and the pastry is cooked
through. Cut into slices while still hot,
then allow to cool.

Sticky Date and Apple Bars

If possible, allow this mixture to mature for 1–2 days before cutting – it will get stickier and better!

MAKES ABOUT 16 BARS

115g/4oz/½ cup margarine
50g/2oz/¼ cup soft dark brown sugar
50g/2oz/4 tbsp golden (light corn) syrup
115g/4oz/¾ cup chopped dates
115g/4oz/generous 1 cup rolled oats
115g/4oz/1 cup self-raising (self-rising)
    wholemeal (whole-wheat) flour
225g/8oz eating apples, peeled, cored and
    grated, and sprinkled with
    5–10ml/1–2 tsp lemon juice
20–25 walnut halves

Nutritional information	
Calories	183kcals/763kJ
Fat	10.11g
Saturated fat	1.64g
Cholesterol	0.14mg
Fibre	1g

1 Preheat the oven to 190°C/375°F/ Gas 5. Line an 18–20cm/7–8in square or rectangular loose-based cake tin (pan) with baking parchment. In a large pan, heat the margarine, sugar, syrup and dates, stirring until the dates soften completely.

2 Gradually work in the oats, flour and apples until well mixed. Spoon into the tin and spread out evenly. Top with the walnut halves.

3 Bake for 30 minutes, then reduce the temperature to 160°C/325°F/Gas 3 and bake for 10–20 minutes more, until firm to the touch and golden.

Apricot Sponge Bars

These fingers are delicious at any time – the apricots keep them moist for several days.

3 Spoon the mixture into the tin, spreading it to the edges, then sprinkle over the flaked almonds.

MAKES 18

225g/8oz/2 cups self-raising (self-rising) flour

115g/4oz/½ cup soft light brown sugar

50g/2oz/⅓ cup semolina

175g/6oz/¾ cup ready-to-eat dried
    apricots, chopped

30ml/2 tbsp clear honey

30ml/2 tbsp malt extract

2 eggs, beaten

60ml/4 tbsp skimmed milk

60ml/4 tbsp sunflower oil

a few drops of almond extract

30ml/2 tbsp flaked (sliced) almonds

1 Preheat the oven to 160°C/325°F/
Gas 3. Lightly grease and then line an
18 x 28cm/7 x 11in baking tin (pan).

4 Bake for 30–35 minutes, or until the centre springs back when pressed. Remove from the tin and turn on to a wire rack to cool. Cut into 18 slices.

Nutritional information

Calories	153
Fat	4.5g
Saturated fat	0.61g
Cholesterol	21.5mg
Fibre	1.27g

2 Sift the flour into a bowl and mix in the sugar, semolina and apricots. Make a well in the centre and add the honey, malt extract, eggs, milk, oil and almond extract. Mix the ingredients together thoroughly until a smooth mixture is reached.

Cook's Tip

Instead of pre-soaked apricots, use chopped dried apricots. Soak in boiling water for 1 hour, drain; add to the mixture.

Apricot Yogurt Cookies

These soft cookies have a lovely texture; they are very quick to make and are useful for lunch boxes.

1 Preheat the oven to 190°C/375°F/
Gas 5. Lightly grease a large
baking sheet.

2 Sift together the flour, baking
powder and cinnamon. Stir in the
oats, sugar, apricots and nuts.

3 Beat together the yogurt and oil,
then stir evenly into the mixture
to make a firm dough. If necessary,
add a little more yogurt.

4 Use your hands to roll the mixture
into about 16 small balls, place on
the baking sheet and flatten with a fork.

5 Sprinkle with demerara sugar.
Bake the cookies for 15–20 minutes,
or until firm and golden brown. Leave to
cool on a wire rack.

MAKES 16

175g/6oz/1½ cups plain (all-purpose) flour
5ml/1 tsp baking powder
5ml/1 tsp ground cinnamon
75g/3oz/scant 1 cup rolled oats
75g/3oz/⅓ cup light muscovado
    (brown) sugar
115g/4oz/½ cup chopped
    ready-to-eat dried apricots
15ml/1 tbsp flaked (sliced) hazelnuts
    or almonds
about 150g/5oz/⅔ cup natural
    (plain) yogurt
45ml/3 tbsp sunflower oil
demerara (raw) sugar, to sprinkle

Nutritional information	
Calories	95kcals/400kJ
Fat	2.66g
Saturated fat	0.37g
Cholesterol	0.3mg
Fibre	0.94g

Cook's Tip

As these cookies have a moist texture,
they do not keep very well, so it is best to
eat them within two days. However, they
do freeze well. Pack them into plastic bags
and freeze for up to four months. They are
ideal for lunch boxes; just take the cookies
out of the freezer when you need them.

Buttermilk Cookies

These simple cookies are perfect for a mid-morning snack, and they taste good with cheese.

1 Preheat the oven to 220°C/425°F/ Gas 7. Grease a baking sheet. Sift the dry ingredients into a bowl. Rub in the butter or margarine with the fingertips until the mixture resembles crumbs.

2 Gradually pour in the buttermilk, stirring with a fork to form a soft dough.

3 Roll out the cookie dough to about a 1cm/½in thickness.

4 Stamp out 5cm/2in rounds with a pastry (cookie) cutter. Place on the prepared baking sheet and bake for 12–15 minutes, or until golden brown. Serve the cookies warm or at room temperature.

MAKES 15

75g/6oz/1½ cups plain (all-purpose) flour
5ml/1 tsp salt
5ml/1 tsp baking powder
2.5ml/½ tsp bicarbonate of soda (baking soda)
60ml/4 tbsp cold butter or margarine
175ml/6fl oz/¾ cup buttermilk

Nutritional information

Calories	85kcals/359kJ
Fat	3.5g
Saturated fat	0.7g
Cholesterol	0.5mg
Fibre	0.5g

Shortcake

These cookies are delicious served warm with some fresh berries and low-fat crème fraîche.

1 Preheat the oven to 220°C/425°F/ Gas 7. Grease a large baking sheet.

2 Sift the flour, sugar, baking powder and salt into a large mixing bowl.

3 Cut the butter into small pieces and rub into the flour using a pastry blender until the mixture resembles coarse crumbs.

4 Pour in the milk and stir with a fork to form a soft dough.

Variation

For Berry Shortcake, split the biscuits in half while still warm. Top one half with lightly sugared fresh berries such as strawberries, raspberries or blueberries, and sandwich with the other half. Serve with dollops of thick, low-fat crème fraîche or thick low-fat yogurt.

Cook's Tips

• Avoid too much handling of the dough because the heat in your hands can turn the fat oily.
• The shortcake should be cooked until it is a pale golden colour; try not to let it get too brown as it affects the flavour.

5 Roll out the dough to about 5mm/¼in thick. Stamp out rounds with a 6cm/2½in pastry (cookie) cutter. Place on the prepared sheet and bake for about 12 minutes, or until golden. Serve hot or warm.

MAKES 8

165g/5½oz/1⅓ cups plain (all-purpose) flour
30ml/2 tbsp caster (superfine) sugar
15ml/1 tbsp baking powder
0.75ml/⅛ tsp salt
75ml/5 tbsp cold butter, cut in pieces
120ml/4fl oz/½ cup skimmed milk

Nutritional information	
Calories	176kcals/740kJ
Fat	8g
Saturated fat	1.5g
Cholesterol	1mg
Fibre	0.8g

Oaty Crisps

These cookies are very crisp and crunchy – ideal to serve with morning coffee.

MAKES 18

175g/6oz/1½ cups rolled oats

75g/3oz/⅓ cup light muscovado (brown) sugar

1 egg

60ml/4 tbsp sunflower oil

30ml/2 tbsp malt extract

Nutritional information

Calories	86kcals/360kJ
Fat	3.59g
Saturated fat	0.57g
Cholesterol	10.7mg
Fibre	0.66g

1 Preheat the oven to 190°C/375°F/ Gas 5. Lightly grease two baking sheets. Mix the rolled oats and sugar in a bowl, breaking up any lumps in the sugar. Add the egg, sunflower oil and malt extract, mix well, then leave to soak for 15 minutes.

2 Using a teaspoon, place small heaps of the mixture well apart on the prepared baking sheets. Press the heaps into 7.5cm/3in rounds with the back of a dampened fork.

3 Bake the cookies for 10–15 minutes until golden brown. Leave them to cool for 1 minute, then remove with a palette knife or metal spatula and cool on a wire rack. Store in an airtight container for up to 3 days.

Cook's Tip

Oats contain soluble fibre, which helps to lower cholesterol levels. Because oats do not contain gluten, they are suitable for people who are gluten-intolerant.

Variation

To give these cookies a coarser texture, substitute jumbo oats for some or all of the rolled oats. Once cool, store the cookies in an airtight container to keep them crisp and fresh.

Orange Cookies

These light, crispy cookies are a popular choice for a coffee break or a snack at any time.

1 With an electric mixer, cream the butter and sugar until light and fluffy. Add the yolks, orange juice and rind, and continue beating to blend. Set aside.

2 In another bowl, sift together the flours, salt and baking powder. Add to the butter mixture and stir until it forms a dough.

3 Wrap the dough in baking parchment and chill for 2 hours.

4 Preheat the oven to 190°C/375°F/ Gas 5. Grease two baking sheets.

5 Roll spoonfuls of the dough into balls and place 2.5–5cm/1–2in apart on the prepared sheets.

6 Press down with a fork to flatten. Bake for 8–10 minutes, until golden brown. With a metal spatula, transfer to a rack to cool.

MAKES 30

115g/4oz/½ cup butter
200g/7oz/1 cup caster (superfine) sugar
2 egg yolks
15ml/1 tbsp orange juice
grated rind of 1 orange
175g/6oz/1½ cups plain (all-purpose) flour
115g/4oz/½ cup self-raising (self-rising) flour
2.5ml/½ tsp salt
5ml/1 tsp baking powder

Nutritional information	
Calories	84kcals/353kJ
Fat	3.5g
Saturated fat	0.7g
Cholesterol	14mg
Fibre	0.2g

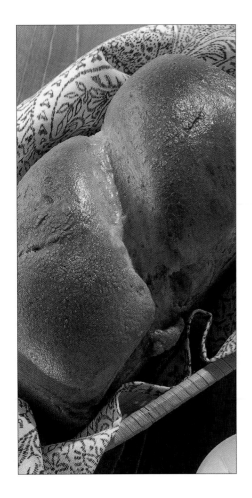

BREADS

The mouthwatering aroma of freshly baked bread is evocative
of home and all good things. As well as being fun to make,
all of these breads taste wonderful. You can indulge in
them yourself, because they are all low in fat.

Austrian Three Grain Bread

A mixture of grains gives this close-textured bread a delightful nutty flavour.
Make two smaller twists, if preferred.

MAKES 1 LOAF

475ml/16fl oz/2 cups warm water
10ml/2 tsp active dried yeast
a pinch of sugar
225g/8oz/2 cups strong white bread flour
7.5ml/1½ tsp salt
225g/8oz/2 cups malted brown flour
225g/8oz/2 cups rye flour
30ml/2 tbsp linseed
75g/3oz/¾ cup medium oatmeal
45ml/3 tbsp sunflower seeds
30ml/2 tbsp malt extract

Nutritional information

Calories	367kcals/1540kJ
Fat	5.36g
Saturated fat	0.6g
Cholesterol	0mg
Fibre	6.67g

Cook's Tip

For all bread recipes that call for yeast, use strong bread flour rather than plain (all-purpose) or self-raising (self-rising) flour. Strong bread flours have a high gluten content, which is important to allow the action of the yeast to aerate the dough. When the dough is baked, bubbles of gas trapped in the dough during the fermentation process produce a light and airy effect. When the bread is sliced, it will have a spongy appearance due to the tiny holes.

1 Put half the water in a jug (pitcher). Sprinkle the yeast on top. Add the sugar, mix well and leave for 10 minutes.

2 Sift the white flour and salt into a mixing bowl and add the other flours. Set aside 5ml/1 tsp of the linseed and add the rest to the flour mixture with the oatmeal and sunflower seeds. Make a well in the centre. Add the yeast mixture to the bowl with the malt extract and the remaining water.

3 Gradually incorporate the flour and mix to a soft dough, adding extra water if necessary.

4 On a floured surface, knead for 5 minutes until smooth and elastic. Return to the bowl and cover. Leave for 2 hours until doubled in bulk.

5 Grease a baking sheet. Turn the dough on to a floured surface, knead for 2 minutes, then divide in half. Roll each half into a 30cm/12in long sausage.

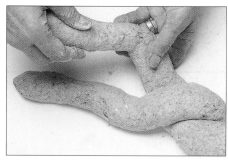

6 Twist the two sausages together, dampen the ends and press to seal. Lift the twist on to the prepared baking sheet. Brush the loaf with water, sprinkle with the remaining linseed and cover loosely with a large plastic bag (ballooning it to trap the air inside). Leave in a warm place until well risen. Preheat the oven to 220°C/425°F/Gas 7.

7 Bake the loaf for 10 minutes, then lower the oven temperature to 200°C/400°F/Gas 6 and cook for 20 minutes more, or until the loaf sounds hollow when it is tapped. Transfer to a wire rack to cool completely.

Irish Soda Bread

This is a solid bread that makes a delicious accompaniment to soups, salads and pickles.

1 Preheat the oven to 200°C/400°F/
Gas 6. Grease a baking sheet.

2 Sift the flours, bicarbonate of soda
and salt together in a bowl. Make a
well in the centre and add the butter
or margarine and buttermilk. Working
outward from the centre, stir with a
fork to combine the ingredients until
a soft dough is formed.

3 With floured hands, gather the
dough into a ball.

4 Transfer to a floured surface and
knead for 3 minutes. Shape the
dough into a large round.

5 Place on the baking sheet. Cut a
cross in the top with a sharp knife.

6 Dust with flour. Bake until brown,
for 40–50 minutes or until the loaf
is well risen and sounds hollow when
tapped on the base. Cool on a wire rack.

Cook's Tip

The addition of buttermilk provides the
acidity that acts with the bicarbonate of
soda, thus helping the bread to rise.

MAKES 1 LOAF

225g/8oz/2 cups plain
(all-purpose) flour
225g/8oz/1 cup plain (all-purpose)
wholemeal (whole-wheat) flour
5ml/1 tsp bicarbonate of soda
(baking soda)
5ml/1 tsp salt
30ml/2 tbsp butter or margarine, melted
350ml/12fl oz/1½ cups buttermilk
15ml/1 tbsp flour, for dusting

Nutritional information	
Calories	188kcals/797kJ
Fat	3.3g
Saturated fat	0.7g
Cholesterol	1mg
Fibre	2.3g

Sage Soda Bread

This tasty loaf, unlike bread made with yeast, has a velvety texture and a powerful aroma of sage.

1 Preheat the oven to 220°C/425°F/ Gas 7. Sift the dry ingredients into a mixing bowl.

2 Stir in the sage and add enough buttermilk to make a soft dough.

3 Shape the dough into a round and place on a lightly oiled baking sheet.

4 Cut a cross in the top, deep into the dough. Bake in the oven for about 40 minutes, or until the loaf is well risen and sounds hollow when tapped on the base. Leave to cool on a wire rack.

MAKES 1 LOAF

175g/6oz/1½ cups plain (all-purpose) wholemeal (whole-wheat) flour
115g/4oz/1 cup strong white bread flour
2.5ml/½ tsp salt
5ml/1 tsp bicarbonate of soda (baking soda)
30ml/2 tbsp shredded fresh sage or 10ml/2 tsp dried sage
300–450ml/½–¾ pint/1¼–scant 2 cups buttermilk

Nutritional information	
Calories	125kcals/525kJ
Fat	9.2g
Saturated fat	0.2g
Cholesterol	0.7mg
Fibre	2.8g

Variation

As an alternative to the sage, try using other herbs, such as finely chopped rosemary or thyme.

Cheese Bread

This is a tasty bread, which would be perfect for making savoury sandwiches.

MAKES 1 LOAF

10ml/2 tsp active dried yeast
250ml/8fl oz/1 cup lukewarm
   skimmed milk
25g/1oz/2 tbsp butter
350g/12oz/3 cups strong white bread flour
10ml/2 tsp salt
115g/4oz/1 cup grated mature
   (sharp) Cheddar cheese

Nutritional information	
Calories	214kcals/903kJ
Fat	4.8g
Saturated fat	1.57g
Cholesterol	5.5mg
Fibre	1.4g

1 Combine the yeast and milk, stir, and leave for 15 minutes to dissolve. Melt the butter, leave to cool, and add to the yeast mixture.

2 Mix the flour and salt together in a large bowl. Make a well in the centre and pour in the yeast mixture. With a wooden spoon, stir from the centre, incorporating flour with each turn, to obtain a rough dough. If the dough seems too dry, add 30–45ml/2–3 tbsp water.

3 Transfer the dough to a floured surface and knead until it is smooth and elastic. Return the dough to the bowl, cover with clear film (plastic wrap) and leave to rise in a warm place until doubled in volume, for 2–3 hours.

4 Grease a 23 x 13cm/9 x 5in loaf tin (pan). Knock back (punch down) the dough with your fist. Knead in the cheese thoroughly.

5 Twist the dough and place in the tin, tucking the ends under. Leave to stand in a warm place until the dough rises above the rim of the tin.

6 Preheat the oven to 200°C/400°F/ Gas 6. Bake for 15 minutes, lower the heat to 190°C/375°F/Gas 5 and bake for about 30 minutes more, until the base sounds hollow when tapped. Cool on a wire rack.

Prosciutto and Parmesan Bread

This nourishing bread will make a satisfying light lunch or supper when served with soup.

2 Mix the mustard and buttermilk together, pour into the flour and quickly mix to a soft dough.

3 Transfer the dough to a floured surface and knead briefly. Shape into an oval loaf, brush with milk and sprinkle with the reserved Parmesan cheese. Put the loaf on the prepared baking sheet.

MAKES 1 LOAF

225g/8oz/2 cups self-raising (self-rising) wholemeal (whole-wheat) flour
225g/8oz/2 cups self-raising (self-rising) white flour
5ml/1 tsp baking powder
5ml/1 tsp salt
5ml/1 tsp black pepper
75g/3oz prosciutto, finely chopped
25g/1oz/⅓ cup freshly grated Parmesan cheese
30ml/2 tbsp chopped fresh parsley
45ml/3 tbsp Meaux mustard
350ml/12fl oz/1½ cups buttermilk
skimmed milk, to glaze

1 Preheat the oven to 200°C/400°F/ Gas 6. Flour a baking sheet. Place the wholemeal flour in a bowl and sift in the white flour, baking powder and salt. Add the pepper and the prosciutto. Set aside about 15ml/ 1 tbsp of the grated Parmesan and stir the rest into the flour mixture with the parsley. Make a well in the centre of the dry ingredients.

4 Bake the loaf for 25–30 minutes, or until it sounds hollow when tapped on the base. Allow to cool on a wire rack before slicing and serving.

Nutritional information

Calories	250kcals/1054kJ
Fat	3.7g
Saturated fat	1.3g
Cholesterol	7mg
Fibre	3.8g

Olive and Herb Bread

Olive breads are popular all over the Mediterranean. For this Greek recipe, use rich, oily olives.

3 Transfer to a lightly floured surface and knead for about 10 minutes. Put in a clean bowl, cover with clear film (plastic wrap) and leave in a warm place until doubled in size.

4 Preheat the oven to 220°C/425°F/ Gas 7. Lightly grease two baking sheets. Turn the dough on to a floured surface and cut in half. Shape into two rounds and place on the baking sheets. Cover loosely with lightly oiled clear film and leave until doubled in size.

5 Slash the tops of the loaves with a knife, then bake for about 40 minutes or until the loaves sound hollow when tapped on the base. Transfer to a wire rack to cool.

MAKES 2 LOAVES

2 red onions, thinly sliced

30ml/2 tbsp olive oil

225g/8oz/2 cups pitted black or green olives, in oil and herbs

800g/1¾lb/7 cups strong white bread flour

7.5ml/1½ tsp salt

20ml/4 tsp easy-blend (rapid-rise) dried yeast

45ml/3 tbsp roughly chopped parsley, coriander (cilantro) or mint

457ml/16fl oz/2 cups hand-hot water

1 Fry the onions in the oil until soft. Roughly chop the olives.

2 Put the flour, salt, yeast and parsley, coriander or mint in a large bowl with the olives and fried onions and pour in the water. Mix to a dough using a round-bladed knife, adding a little more water if the mixture feels dry.

Nutritional information

Calories	157kcals/664kJ
Fat	2.9g
Saturated fat	0.41g
Cholesterol	0mg
Fibre	1.8g

Variation

Shape the dough into 16 small rolls. Slash the tops as above and reduce the cooking time to 25 minutes.

Dill Bread

Home-made herb bread, fresh from the oven, is a tasty addition to a light lunch or supper.

1 Mix together the yeast, water and sugar in a large bowl and leave for 15 minutes to dissolve.

2 Stir in 350g/12oz/3 cups of the flour. Cover and leave to rise in a warm place for 45 minutes.

3 Cook the onion in 15ml/1 tbsp of the oil until soft. Set aside to cool, then stir into the yeast mixture. Stir the dill, eggs, cottage cheese, salt and remaining oil into the yeast mixture. Gradually add the remaining flour until too stiff to stir. Put on a floured surface.

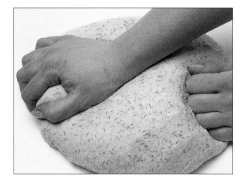

4 Knead until smooth and elastic. Place in a bowl, cover, and leave to rise for 1½ hours until doubled in size.

5 Grease a large baking sheet. Cut the dough in half and shape into two rounds. Place on the baking sheet and leave to rise in a warm place for 30 minutes.

6 Preheat the oven to 190°C/375°F/ Gas 5. Score the tops, brush with the milk, and bake until browned and the base sound hollow when tapped, about 50 minutes. Cool on a rack.

MAKES 2 LOAVES

20ml/4 tsp active dried yeast
475ml/16fl oz/2 cups lukewarm water
30ml/2 tbsp caster (superfine) sugar
850g/1lb 14oz/7½ cups strong
    white bread flour
½ onion, chopped
60ml/4 tbsp vegetable oil
a large bunch of dill, finely chopped
2 eggs, lightly beaten
115g/4oz/½ cup cottage cheese
20ml/4 tsp salt
milk, for glazing

Nutritional information

Calories	237kcals/1003kJ
Fat	3.7g
Saturated fat	0.6g
Cholesterol	20mg
Fibre	1.8g

Squash and Nut Loaf

This moist and crunchy loaf, which is made with courgette and walnuts, is a good teatime treat.

1 Preheat the oven to 180°C/350°F/ Gas 4. Grease the base and sides of a 900g/2lb loaf tin (pan) and line with baking parchment.

2 Beat the eggs and sugar together and gradually add the oil.

3 Sift the flour into a bowl together with the baking powder, bicarbonate of soda, cinnamon and allspice.

4 Mix in the egg mixture with the rest of the ingredients, reserving 15ml/ 1 tbsp of the sunflower seeds for the top.

5 Spoon into the loaf tin, level off the top, and sprinkle with the reserved sunflower seeds.

6 Bake for about 1 hour or until a skewer inserted in the centre comes out clean. Leave to cool slightly, then turn out on to a wire cooling rack.

MAKES 1 LOAF

3 eggs
75g/3oz/⅓ cup soft light brown sugar
50ml/2fl oz/¼ cup sunflower oil
225g/8oz/2 cups plain (all-purpose) wholemeal (whole-wheat) flour
5ml/1 tsp baking powder
5ml/1 tsp bicarbonate of soda (baking soda)
5ml/1 tsp ground cinnamon
2.5ml/½ tsp ground allspice
7.5ml/1½ tsp green cardamoms, seeds removed and crushed
150g/5oz/1 cup coarsely grated courgette (zucchini)
50g/2oz/½ cup walnuts, chopped
50g/2oz/⅓ cup sunflower seeds

Nutritional information

Calories	307kcals/1290kJ
Fat	20.19g
Saturated fat	2.64g
Cholesterol	65.45mg
Fibre	2.86g

Oatmeal Bread

A healthy bread with a delightfully crumbly texture due to the addition of rolled oats.

MAKES 2 LOAVES

475ml/16fl oz/2 cups skimmed milk
25g/1oz/2 tbsp low-fat margarine
50g/2oz/¼ cup soft dark brown sugar
10ml/2 tsp salt
15ml/1 tbsp easy-blend (rapid-rise)
    dried yeast
50ml/2fl oz/¼ cup lukewarm water
400g/14oz/4 cups rolled oats
450–675g/1–1½lb/4–6 cups
    strong white bread flour

Nutritional information

Calories	228kcals/958kJ
Fat	3.44g
Saturated fat	1.19g
Cholesterol	3.9mg
Fibre	2.41g

1 Scald the milk. Remove from the heat and stir in the margarine, sugar and salt. Set aside until lukewarm.

2 Combine the yeast and lukewarm water in a large bowl and leave until the yeast is dissolved and the mixture is frothy. Stir in the milk mixture.

3 Add 275g/10oz/3 cups of the oats and 450g/1lb/4 cups of the flour. Work it into the milk mixture, adding more flour until you have a soft and pliable dough.

4 Transfer to a floured surface and knead until the dough is smooth and elastic.

5 Place the dough in a greased bowl, cover with a plastic bag, and leave for about 2–3 hours, until doubled in volume. Grease a large baking sheet.

6 Transfer the dough to a lightly floured surface and divide in half.

7 Shape into rounds. Place on the baking sheet, cover with a damp dish towel and leave to rise for about 1 hour, until doubled in volume.

8 Score the tops of the loaves and sprinkle with the remaining oats. Bake for about 45–50 minutes, until the bottoms sound hollow when tapped. Cool on wire racks.

Rosemary and Sea Salt Focaccia

Focaccia is an Italian flat bread made with olive oil. Here, rosemary and coarse sea salt add flavour.

MAKES 1 LOAF

350g/12oz/3 cups strong white bread flour

2.5ml/½ tsp salt

10ml/2 tsp easy-blend (rapid-rise)
   dried yeast

250ml/8fl oz/1 cup lukewarm water

45ml/3 tbsp olive oil

1 small red onion

leaves from 1 large rosemary sprig

5ml/1 tsp coarse sea salt

Nutritional information	
Calories	191kcals/807kJ
Fat	4.72g
Saturated fat	0.68g
Cholesterol	0mg
Fibre	1.46g

1 Sift the flour and salt into a large mixing bowl. Stir in the yeast, then make a well in the middle of the dry ingredients. Pour in the water and 30ml/2 tbsp of the oil. Mix well, adding a little more water if the mixture seems too dry.

2 Transfer the dough to a lightly floured surface and knead for about 10 minutes until smooth and elastic.

3 Place the dough in a greased bowl, cover and leave in a warm place for about 1 hour until doubled in size. Knock back (punch down) and knead the dough for 2–3 minutes.

4 Meanwhile, preheat the oven to 220°C/425°F/Gas 7 and lightly grease a baking sheet. Roll out the dough to a large circle about 1cm/½in thick, and transfer to the baking sheet. Brush with the remaining oil.

Cook's Tips

The dimpling on the top of the dough is achieved by simply pushing the fingers into it after adding the topping ingredients. The indentations that are made collect the oil and allow it to seep into the bread. A good focaccia should be full of flavour and light. It can be eaten on its own or used for tasty grilled sand-wiches or classic paninis.

Variation

If you are short of time, you can use a packet mix to make this bread. Just follow the instructions, then add the olive oil, onion and rosemary, knead and leave to rise. Continue from step 3 in the recipe, omitting step 5.

5 Halve the onion and slice it thinly. Sprinkle over the dough with the rosemary and sea salt, pressing lightly.

6 Make indentations in the dough with your finger. Cover with greased clear film (plastic wrap) and leave the dough to rise in a warm place for 30 minutes. Remove the clear film and bake for 25–30 minutes until golden.

Saffron Focaccia

This dazzling yellow bread is light in texture and the saffron lends it a distinctive flavour.

MAKES 1 LOAF

a pinch of saffron threads
150ml/¼ pint/⅔ cup boiling water
225g/8oz/2 cups strong white bread flour
2.5ml/½ tsp salt
5ml/1 tsp easy-blend (rapid-rise)
    dried yeast
15ml/1 tbsp olive oil

For the topping

2 garlic cloves, sliced
1 red onion, cut into thin wedges
rosemary sprigs
12 pitted black olives, coarsely chopped
15ml/1 tbsp olive oil

Nutritional information

Calories	104kcals/439kJ
Fat	15.91g
Saturated fat	4g
Cholesterol	0mg
Fibre	9.4g

Cook's Tips

• Saffron is the world's most expensive spice, but fortunately, only a small amount is needed because it is both pungent and aromatic. To obtain the maximum colour and flavour, it is best to infuse the saffron threads first in a little boiling water or stock.
• Saffron is also available as a powder, but this form of the spice tends to lose its flavour and it can be easily adulterated.
• To store saffron, keep in a cool, dark place for up to six months.
• Focaccia can be eaten as a snack or as an accompaniment to salads and soups.

1 Infuse the saffron in the boiling water. Set aside until it has cooled to lukewarm.

2 Place the flour, salt, yeast and olive oil in a food processor. Turn on and gradually add the saffron and its liquid until the dough forms a ball.

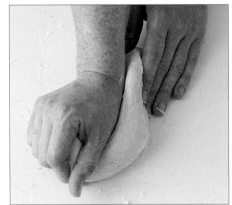

3 Transfer to a floured board and knead for 10–15 minutes. Place in a bowl, cover and leave to rise for about 30–40 minutes, until doubled in size.

4 Knock back (punch down) the risen dough on a lightly floured surface then roll it out into an oval shape, about 1cm/½in thick. Place the dough on a lightly greased baking sheet and leave to rise for 20–30 minutes.

5 Preheat the oven to 200°C/400°F/ Gas 6. Use your fingers to press small indentations in the dough.

6 Sprinkle the topping ingredients over the dough then brush all over lightly with olive oil, and bake the focaccia for about 25 minutes or until the loaf sounds hollow when tapped on the base. Leave to cool on a wire rack.

Naan

Serve naan as soon as they are made, if possible; otherwise, wrap them in foil to keep warm.

MAKES 6

5ml/1 tsp caster (superfine) sugar
5ml/1 tsp dried yeast
150ml/¼ pint/⅔ cup lukewarm water
225g/8oz/2 cups strong white bread flour
5ml/1 tsp ghee or butter
5ml/1 tsp salt
50g/2oz/¼ cup low-fat margarine, melted
5ml/1 tsp poppy seeds

Nutritional information	
Calories	177kcals/744kJ
Fat	5.07g
Saturated fat	1.24g
Cholesterol	0.5mg
Fibre	0.2g

1 Put the sugar and yeast in a small bowl, add the warm water and mix well until the yeast has dissolved. Leave for 10 minutes or until the mixture becomes frothy.

2 Place the flour in a large mixing bowl, make a well in the middle, and add the ghee or butter and the salt, then pour in the yeast mixture.

3 Mix well, using your hands, to make a dough, adding some more water if the dough is too dry. Turn out on to a floured surface and knead for about 5 minutes or until smooth.

4 Place the dough back in the clean bowl, cover with foil and leave to rise in a warm place for 1½ hours or until it has doubled in size.

5 Preheat the grill (broiler) to hot. Knead the dough on a floured surface for a further 2 minutes. Break off small balls and roll into rounds 12cm/ 4½in in diameter and 1cm/½in thick.

6 Place on a sheet of greased foil and grill (broil) for 7–10 minutes, turning twice to brush with margarine and sprinkle with poppy seeds.

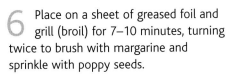

Country Bread

This loaf is high in fibre and low in fat, and is made with a mixture of wholemeal and white flour.

1 For the starter, combine the yeast, water, flour and sugar in a bowl and stir with a fork. Cover and leave in a warm place for 2–3 hours, or leave overnight in a cool place.

2 Place the flours, salt and butter in a food processor and process just until blended, for 1–2 minutes. Stir together the milk and starter, then slowly pour into the processor, with the motor running, until the mixture forms a dough. If necessary, add more water. Alternatively, the dough can be mixed by hand. Transfer to a floured surface and knead until smooth and elastic.

3 Place in an ungreased bowl, cover with a clean plastic bag, and leave to rise in a warm place until doubled in volume, for about 1½ hours. Transfer to a floured surface and knead briefly. Return to the bowl and leave to rise until tripled in volume, about 1½ hours.

5 For each loaf, top the large ball with the small ball and press the centre with the handle of a wooden spoon to secure. Slash the top, cover with a clean plastic bag and leave to rise.

MAKES 2 LOAVES

275g/10oz/2½ cups strong wholemeal (whole-wheat) bread flour
275g/10oz/2½ cups plain (all-purpose) flour
115g/4oz/1 cup strong white bread flour
20ml/4 tsp salt
60ml/4 tbsp butter
475ml/16fl oz/2 cups lukewarm milk

For the starter

10ml/2 tsp dried yeast
250ml/8fl oz/1 cup lukewarm water
115g/4oz/1 cup plain (all-purpose) flour
1.5ml/¼ tsp caster (superfine) sugar

4 Divide the dough in half. Cut off one-third of the dough from each half and shape into balls. Shape the larger remaining pieces into balls. Grease a baking sheet.

6 Preheat the oven to 200°C/400°F/ Gas 6. Dust the loaves with wholemeal flour and bake for about 50 minutes, until the top is browned and the bottom sounds hollow when tapped. Cool on a rack before serving.

Nutritional information

Calories	204kcals/863kJ
Fat	3.3g
Saturated fat	0.6g
Cholesterol	1mg
Fibre	2.7g

Cheese and Onion Sticks

An extremely tasty bread which is very good served with soups or salads. Use an extra-mature cheese to give plenty of flavour without adding more fat.

MAKES 2 LOAVES

300ml/½ pint/1¼ cups warm water
5ml/1 tsp active dried yeast
a pinch of sugar
15ml/1 tbsp sunflower oil
1 red onion, finely chopped
450g/1lb/4 cups strong white bread flour
5ml/1 tsp salt
5ml/1 tsp dry mustard
45ml/3 tbsp chopped fresh herbs, such as
    thyme, parsley, marjoram or sage
75g/3oz/¾ cup grated reduced-fat
    Cheddar cheese

Nutritional information

Calories	210kcals/882kJ
Fat	3.16g
Saturated fat	0.25g
Cholesterol	3.22mg
Fibre	1.79g

Variation

To make Onion and Coriander Sticks, omit the cheese, herbs and mustard. Substitute with 15ml/1 tbsp ground coriander and 45ml/3 tbsp chopped fresh coriander (cilantro).

1 Put the water in a jug (pitcher). Sprinkle the yeast on top. Add the sugar, mix well and leave for 10 minutes.

2 Heat the oil in a small frying pan and fry the onion until it is well coloured.

3 Combine the flour, salt and mustard in a mixing bowl, then add the chopped herbs. Set aside 30ml/2 tbsp of the cheese. Stir the rest into the flour mixture and make a well in the centre. Add the prepared mixture with the fried onions and oil, then gradually incorporate the flour to make a soft dough, adding extra water if necessary. Transfer the dough to a floured surface.

4 Knead for 5 minutes until smooth and elastic. Return to the clean bowl, cover with a damp dish towel and leave in a warm place to rise for about 2 hours, until doubled in bulk. Lightly grease two baking sheets.

5 Transfer the dough to a floured surface and knead briefly. Divide in half and roll each piece into a 30cm/12in long stick. Place the sticks on baking sheets and make cuts along the top.

6 Sprinkle the sticks with the reserved cheese. Cover and leave for 30 minutes until well risen. Preheat the oven to 220°C/425°F/Gas 7. Bake the sticks for 25 minutes or until they sound hollow when tapped underneath. Cool on a wire rack.

Saffron and Basil Breadsticks

Saffron lends its delicate aroma and flavour, as well as rich yellow colour, to these tasty breadsticks.

MAKES 32

a generous pinch of saffron threads
30ml/2 tbsp hot water
450g/1lb/4 cups strong white
    bread flour
5ml/1 tsp salt
10ml/2 tsp easy-blend (rapid-rise)
    dried yeast
300ml/½ pint/1¼ cups lukewarm water
45ml/3 tbsp olive oil
45ml/3 tbsp chopped fresh basil

Nutritional information

Calories	59kcals/249kJ
Fat	1.3g
Saturated fat	1.17g
Cholesterol	0mg
Fibre	0.4g

Cook's Tip

Use powdered saffron if saffron threads are not available. Turmeric is an inexpensive alternative: it imparts a lovely gold colour, but its flavour is not as delicate as saffron.

1 Infuse the saffron threads in the hot water for 10 minutes.

2 Sift the flour and salt into a large mixing bowl. Stir in the yeast, then make a well in the centre of the dry ingredients. Pour in the lukewarm water and the saffron liquid and mix together lightly.

3 Add the olive oil and the chopped basil. Use a wooden spoon and mix to a soft dough. Turn the mixture out on to a lightly floured work surface or board.

4 Knead the dough for about 10 minutes until smooth and elastic. Place in a greased bowl, cover with clear film (plastic wrap) and leave for about 1 hour until it has doubled in size.

5 Knock back (punch down) and knead the dough on a lightly floured surface for 2–3 minutes.

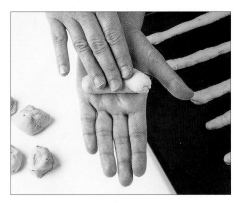

6 Preheat the oven to 220°C/425°F/ Gas 7. Divide the dough into 32 pieces and shape into long sticks. Place well apart on greased baking sheets, then leave for a further 15–20 minutes until they become puffy. Bake for about 15 minutes until crisp and golden. Serve warm.

Sun-dried Tomato Plait

This is a marvellous Mediterranean-flavoured bread to serve at a summer buffet or barbecue.

MAKES 1 LOAF
300ml/½ pint/1¼ cups warm water
5ml/1 tsp dried yeast
a pinch of sugar
225g/8oz/2 cups strong wholemeal
    (whole-wheat) bread flour
225g/8oz/2 cups strong white bread flour
5ml/1 tsp salt
1.5ml/¼ tsp ground black pepper
50g/2oz/⅔ cup drained, chopped sun-dried
    tomatoes in oil, plus 15ml/1 tbsp oil from the jar
25g/1oz/⅓ cup freshly grated
    Parmesan cheese
30ml/2 tbsp red pesto
5ml/1 tsp coarse salt

Nutritional information

Calories	294kcals/1233kJ
Fat	12.12g
Saturated fat	2.13g
Cholesterol	3.4mg
Fibre	3.39g

Cook's Tip
If you are unable to locate red pesto, use 30ml/2 tbsp chopped fresh basil mixed with 15ml/1 tbsp sun-dried tomato purée (paste).

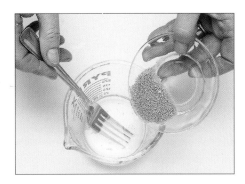

1 Put half the warm water in a jug (pitcher). Add the yeast and sugar, mix well and leave for 10 minutes.

2 Put the wholemeal flour in a mixing bowl. Sift in the white flour, salt and pepper. Make a well in the centre then add the yeast mixture, sun-dried tomatoes, oil, Parmesan, pesto and the remaining water. Gradually incorporate the flour and mix to a soft dough, adding a little extra water if necessary.

3 Transfer the dough to a floured surface and knead for 5 minutes until smooth and elastic. Return to the clean bowl, cover with a damp dish towel and leave in a warm place to rise for about 2 hours until doubled in bulk. Lightly grease a baking sheet.

4 Transfer the dough on to a lightly floured surface and knead for a few minutes. Divide the dough into three equal pieces and shape each into a 30cm/12in long sausage.

5 Dampen the ends of the three sausages. Press them together at one end, plait them loosely, then press them together at the other end. Place on the baking sheet, cover and leave in a warm place for 30 minutes until well risen. Preheat the oven to 220°C/425°F/Gas 7.

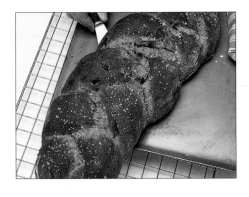

6 Sprinkle the bread with the coarse salt. Bake for 10 minutes, then lower the temperature to 200°C/400°F/Gas 6 and bake for a further 15–20 minutes, or until the loaf sounds hollow when tapped underneath. Cool on a wire rack.

Poppy Seed Rolls

These soft rolls make a welcome change when served for breakfast or with dinner.

MAKES 12

300ml/½ pint/1¼ cups warm skimmed milk
5ml/1 tsp active dried yeast
a pinch of sugar
450g/1lb/4 cups strong white bread flour
5ml/1 tsp salt
1 egg

For the topping

1 egg, beaten
poppy seeds

Nutritional information

Calories	160kcals/674kJ
Fat	2.42g
Saturated fat	0.46g
Cholesterol	32.58mg
Fibre	1.16g

Variations

Use easy-blend (rapid rise) dried yeast if you prefer. Add it directly to the dry ingredients and mix with hand-hot milk. The rolls will only require one rising (*see* yeast package instructions). Vary the toppings. Linseed, sesame seeds and caraway seeds are all good; try adding caraway seeds as well for extra flavour.

1 Put half the warm milk in a small bowl. Sprinkle the yeast on top. Add the sugar, mix well and leave to stand for 30 minutes.

2 Sift the flour and salt into a mixing bowl. Make a well in the centre and pour in the yeast mixture and the egg. Gradually incorporate the flour, adding enough of the remaining milk to mix to a soft dough.

3 Turn the dough on to a floured surface and knead for 5 minutes until smooth and elastic. Return to the clean bowl, cover with a damp dish towel and leave in a warm place to rise for about 1 hour until doubled in bulk.

4 Lightly grease two baking sheets. Turn the dough on to a floured surface. Knead for 2 minutes, then cut into 12 pieces and shape into rolls.

5 Place the rolls on the prepared baking sheets, cover loosely with a large plastic bag (ballooning it to trap the air inside) and leave to stand in a warm place until the rolls have risen well. Preheat the oven to 220°C/425°F/Gas 7.

6 Glaze the rolls with the beaten egg, sprinkle with poppy seeds and bake for 12–15 minutes until golden brown. Transfer to a wire rack to cool. Serve when the rolls are still just warm, or once they have cooled down.

Clover Leaf Rolls

These novelty rolls are sure to become a firm favourite with your family and friends.

1 Heat the milk until lukewarm. Pour into a large bowl and stir in the sugar, butter and yeast. Leave for 15 minutes.

2 Stir the egg and salt into the yeast mixture. Gradually stir in 350g/ 12oz/3 cups of the flour. Add just enough extra flour to obtain a rough dough.

3 Knead on a floured surface until smooth and elastic. Place in a greased bowl, cover, and leave in a warm place until doubled in volume, about 1½ hours. Grease two 12-cup muffin tins (pans).

4 Knock back (punch down) the dough. Cut into four pieces. Roll each piece into a rope 35cm/14in long. Cut each rope into 18 pieces, then roll each into a ball.

5 Place three balls, side by side, in each muffin cup. Cover loosely and leave to rise in a warm place for about half an hour, until doubled in volume.

6 Preheat the oven to 200°C/400°F/ Gas 6. Brush the rolls with melted butter. Bake for about 20 minutes, until lightly browned. Cool on a wire rack.

MAKES 24

300ml/½ pint/1¼ cups skimmed milk
30ml/2 tbsp caster (superfine) sugar
50g/2oz/¼ cup butter
10ml/2 tsp active dried yeast
1 egg
10ml/2 tsp salt
350–450g/12oz–1lb/3–4 cups strong white
    bread flour
melted butter, for glazing

Nutritional information	
Calories	109kcals/459kJ
Fat	2.9g
Saturated fat	0.6g
Cholesterol	8mg
Fibre	0.7g

Wholemeal Buttermilk Rolls

These traditional wholemeal rolls are made with buttermilk to keep the fat content low.

MAKES 12

10ml/2 tsp active dried yeast
50ml/2fl oz/¼ cup lukewarm water
5ml/1 tsp caster (superfine) sugar
175ml/6fl oz/¾ cup lukewarm buttermilk
1.5ml/¼ tsp bicarbonate of soda
    (baking soda)
5ml/1 tsp salt
40g/1½oz/3 tbsp butter
185g/6½oz/1⅔ cups strong wholemeal
    (whole-wheat) bread flour
about 115g/4oz/1 cup strong white bread flour
1 beaten egg, for glazing

Nutritional information

Calories	143kcals/603kJ
Fat	4.2g
Saturated fat	0.8g
Cholesterol	17mg
Fibre	2.1g

1 In a large bowl, combine the yeast, water and sugar. Stir, and leave for 15 minutes to dissolve.

2 Add the buttermilk, bicarbonate of soda, salt and butter and stir to blend. Stir in the wholemeal flour.

3 Add just enough of the white flour to obtain a rough dough. If the dough is stiff, stir it with your hands.

4 Transfer to a floured surface and knead until smooth and elastic. Divide into three equal parts. Roll each into a cylinder, then cut into four.

5 Form the pieces into torpedo shapes. Place on a greased baking sheet, cover, and leave in a warm place until doubled in volume.

6 Preheat the oven to 200°C/400°F/ Gas 6. Brush with the glaze. Bake for 15–20 minutes, until firm. Allow to cool.

Cook's Tip

Buttermilk is low-fat milk which has a special culture added that causes fermentation under controlled conditions. The result is a thickened texture and a tangy, slightly acidic flavour, which is perfect for rolls and scones.

Index